# CAMBRIDGE
# Primary Mathematics

## Workbook 2

Cherri Moseley & Janet Rees

# CAMBRIDGE
## UNIVERSITY PRESS

Shaftesbury Road, Cambridge CB2 8EA, United Kingdom

One Liberty Plaza, 20th Floor, New York, NY 10006, USA

477 Williamstown Road, Port Melbourne, VIC 3207, Australia

314–321, 3rd Floor, Plot 3, Splendor Forum, Jasola District Centre, New Delhi – 110025, India

103 Penang Road, #05-06/07, Visioncrest Commercial, Singapore 238467

Cambridge University Press is part of the University of Cambridge.

It furthers the University's mission by disseminating knowledge in the pursuit of education, learning and research at the highest international levels of excellence.

www.cambridge.org
Information on this title: www.cambridge.org/9781108746465

© Cambridge University Press & Assessment 2021

This publication is in copyright. Subject to statutory exception and to the provisions of relevant collective licensing agreements, no reproduction of any part may take place without the written permission of Cambridge University Press.

First published 2021

20

Printed in the Netherlands by Wilco BV

*A catalogue record for this publication is available from the British Library*

ISBN 978-1-108-74646-5 Workbook with Digital Access (1 Year)

Additional resources for this publication at www.cambridge.org/9781108746465

Cambridge University Press has no responsibility for the persistence or accuracy of URLs for external or third-party internet websites referred to in this publication, and does not guarantee that any content on such websites is, or will remain, accurate or appropriate. Information regarding prices, travel timetables, and other factual information given in this work is correct at the time of first printing but Cambridge University Press does not guarantee the accuracy of such information thereafter.

..........................................................................................................................

NOTICE TO TEACHERS
It is illegal to reproduce any part of this work in material form (including photocopying and electronic storage) except under the following circumstances:
(i) where you are abiding by a licence granted to your school or institution by the Copyright Licensing Agency;
(ii) where no such licence exists, or where you wish to exceed the terms of a licence, and you have gained the written permission of Cambridge University Press;
(iii) where you are allowed to reproduce without permission under the provisions of Chapter 3 of the Copyright, Designs and Patents Act 1988, which covers, for example, the reproduction of short passages within certain types of educational anthology and reproduction for the purposes of setting examination questions.

# Contents

| | |
|---|---|
| How to use this book | 5 |
| Thinking and Working Mathematically | 6 |

### 1 Numbers to 100 — 8
1.1 Numbers to 100 — 8
1.2 Counting up to 100 objects — 15
1.3 Comparing and ordering numbers — 22

### 2 Geometry — 27
2.1 3D shapes — 27
2.2 2D shapes and symmetry — 39
2.3 Fractions of shapes — 44

### 3 Measures — 53
3.1 Length — 53
3.2 Drawing and measuring lines — 64

### 4 Statistics — 72
4.1 Carroll diagrams and tally charts — 72

### 5 Working with numbers to 100 — 78
5.1 Addition — 78
5.2 Subtraction — 86
5.3 Multiplication — 94
5.4 Division — 102

### 6 Money — 109
6.1 Money — 109

### 7 Time — 116
7.1 Units of time and the calendar — 116

## Contents

| | | |
|---|---|---|
| **8** | **Numbers to 100 (2)** | **124** |
| 8.1 | Numbers in words, rounding and regrouping | 124 |
| 8.2 | Fractions of numbers | 130 |
| **9** | **Statistics (2)** | **135** |
| 9.1 | Venn diagrams, lists and tables | 135 |
| 9.2 | Pictograms and block graphs | 144 |
| **10** | **Calculating** | **152** |
| 10.1 | Adding and subtracting two 2-digit numbers | 152 |
| 10.2 | Connecting addition and subtraction | 159 |
| 10.3 | Multiplication | 167 |
| 10.4 | Division | 171 |
| **11** | **Geometry (2)** | **175** |
| 11.1 | Angles and turns | 175 |
| 11.2 | Circles | 185 |
| **12** | **Telling the time** | **187** |
| 12.1 | Telling the time | 187 |
| **13** | **Measures (2)** | **194** |
| 13.1 | Mass and temperature | 194 |
| 13.2 | Capacity | 210 |
| **14** | **Pattern and probability** | **217** |
| 14.1 | Pattern and probability | 217 |
| **15** | **Symmetry, position and movement** | **223** |
| 15.1 | Symmetry, position and movement | 223 |
| **Acknowledgements** | | **231** |

# How to use this book

This workbook provides questions for you to practise what you have learned in class. There is a unit to match each unit in your Learner's Book. Each exercise is divided into three parts:

- **Focus:** these questions help you to master the basics
- **Practice:** these questions help you to become more confident in using what you have learned
- **Challenge:** these questions will make you think more deeply.

You might not need to work on all of them. Your teacher will tell you which parts to do.

You will also find these features:

Important words that you will use. ⟶ column   digit   place holder   representation   row

Step-by-step examples showing a way to solve a problem.
There are often many different ways to solve a problem. ⟶

**Worked example 4**
A number sequence starts at 35. It counts on in tens and stops at 65. What are the numbers in this sequence?

I used a 100 square to help me.

All the numbers have 5 ones. They are all odd.

35, 45, 55, 65.

Answer: 35, 45, 55, 65.

These questions will help ⟶ you develop your skills of thinking and working mathematically.

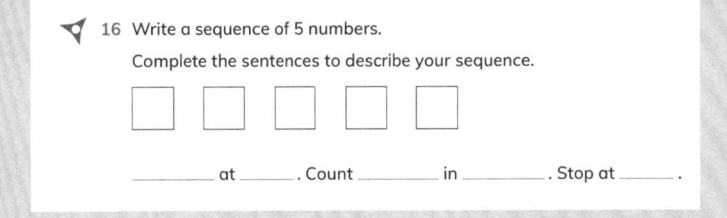

16  Write a sequence of 5 numbers.
Complete the sentences to describe your sequence.

☐ ☐ ☐ ☐ ☐

_____ at _____. Count _____ in _____. Stop at _____.

Thinking and Working Mathematically

# Thinking and Working Mathematically

There are some important skills that you will develop as you learn mathematics.

**Specialising** is when I test examples to see if they fit a rule or pattern.

**Characterising** is when I explain how a group of things are the same.

**Generalising** is when I can explain and use a rule or pattern to find more examples.

**Classifying** is when I put things into groups and can say what rule I have used.

Thinking and Working Mathematically

**Critiquing** is when I think about what is good and what could be better in my work or someone else's work.

**Improving** is when I try to make my maths better.

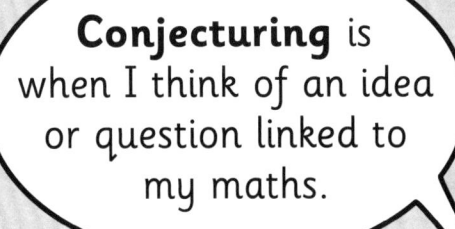

**Conjecturing** is when I think of an idea or question linked to my maths.

**Convincing** is when I explain my thinking to someone else, to help them understand.

# 1 Numbers to 100

## > 1.1 Numbers to 100

> column   digit
> place holder
> representation   row

### Exercise 1.1

**Focus**

1   Write the missing numbers.

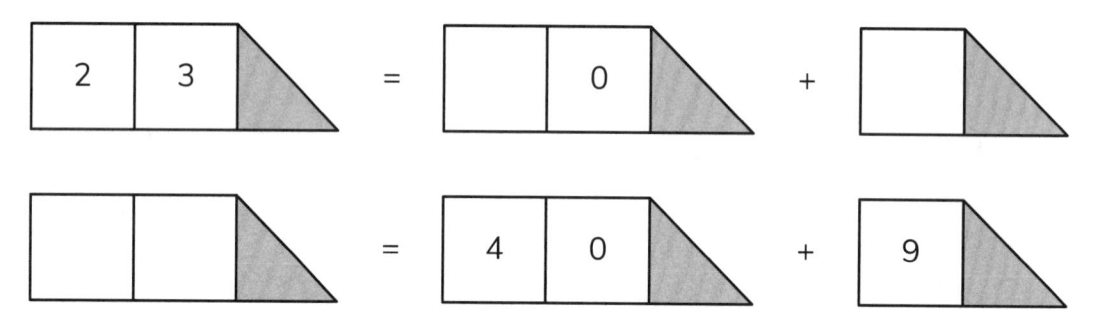

   | 2 | 3 |   =   |   | 0 |   +   |   |

   |   |   |   =   | 4 | 0 |   +   | 9 |

2   Write the missing numbers.

| 21 |  |  |  | 25 |  |  |  |  | 30 |
|---|---|---|---|---|---|---|---|---|---|

| 51 |  |  |  | 55 |  |  |  |  | 60 |
|---|---|---|---|---|---|---|---|---|---|

1.1 Numbers to 100

## Worked example 1

This is a column from the 100 square.

Write the missing numbers.

| |
|---|
| 1 |
| 11 |
| |
| |
| |
| |
| |
| |
| 91 |

Answer:

| |
|---|
| 1 |
| 11 |
| 21 |
| 31 |
| 41 |
| 51 |
| 61 |
| 71 |
| 81 |
| 91 |

Count on in tens. 11, 21, 31, . . . The number of ones stays the same. The number of tens changes.

**1** Numbers to 100

3  Write the missing numbers.

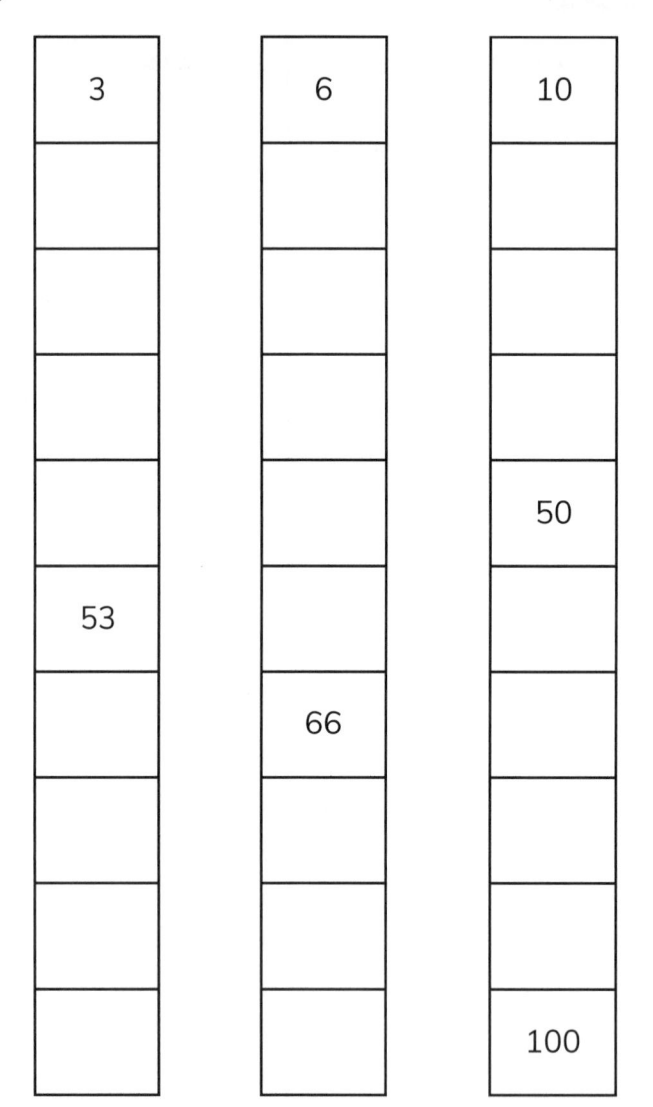

| 3 | | 6 | | 10 |
|---|---|---|---|---|
|   |   |   |   |   |
|   |   |   |   |   |
|   |   |   |   |   |
|   |   |   |   | 50 |
|   |   |   |   |   |
| 53|   |   |   |   |
|   |   | 66|   |   |
|   |   |   |   |   |
|   |   |   |   |   |
|   |   |   |   | 100|

4  Which 2-digit numbers are represented here?

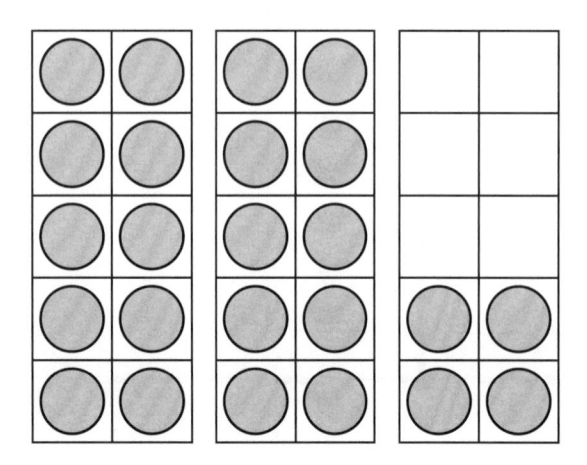

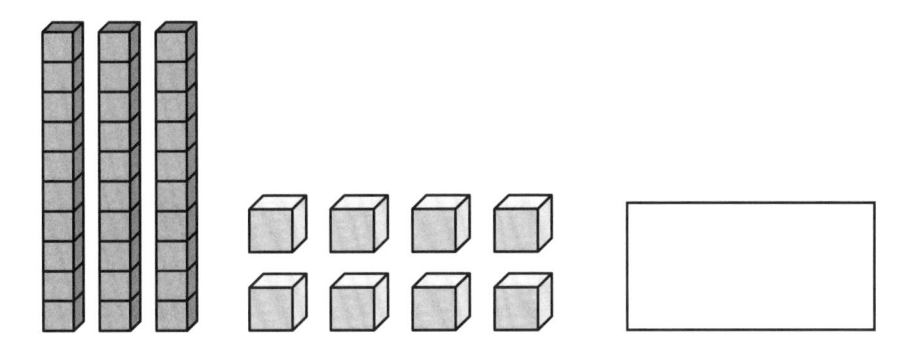

1.1 Numbers to 100

5   Draw a different representation of this number.

Show your representation to a partner or carer.

How is your representation the same as theirs? How is it different?

## Practice

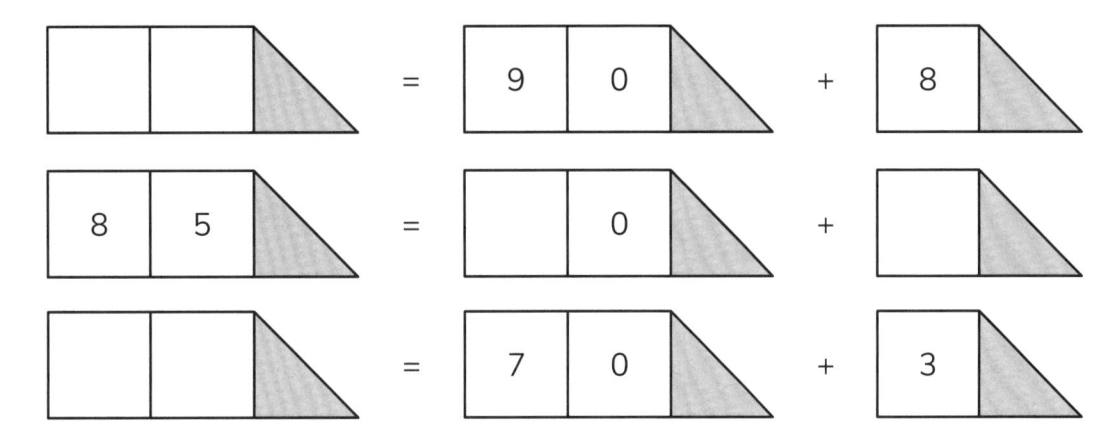

6   Write the missing numbers.

| | | = | 9 | 0 | + | 8 |

| 8 | 5 | = | | 0 | + | |

| | | = | 7 | 0 | + | 3 |

**1** Numbers to 100

7 Here are some rows and columns from a 100 square.

Write the missing numbers.

| | | | | | | | | | 80 |
|---|---|---|---|---|---|---|---|---|---|

| | | | | | | | | | 20 |
|---|---|---|---|---|---|---|---|---|---|

| 4 |
|---|
| |
| |
| |
| |
| |
| |
| 74 |
| |
| |

| 8 |
|---|
| |
| |
| |
| |
| |
| |
| |
| 88 |
| |

1.1 Numbers to 100

8  Draw a representation of 23 and a representation of 32.

How are they the same? How are they different?

Discuss your representations with a partner or carer.

9  Here are some pieces of a 100 square.

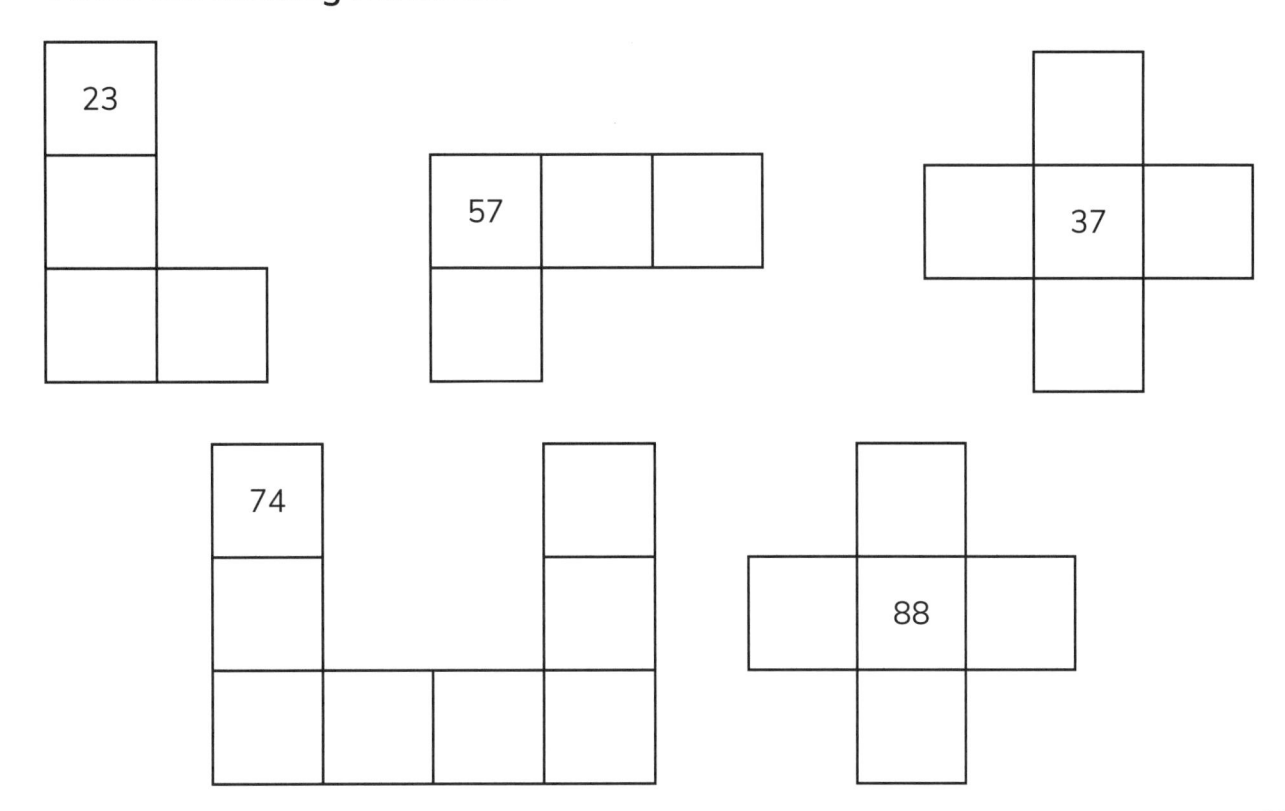

Write the missing numbers.

**1** Numbers to 100

## Challenge

10 Here is a mostly blank 100 square.

Write these numbers in the correct places.

37   81   53   90   75   46   69

|   |   |   |   |   |   |   |   |   |   |
|---|---|---|---|---|---|---|---|---|---|
| 1 |   |   |   |   |   |   |   |   |   |
|   |   |   |   |   |   |   |   |   |   |
|   |   |   |   |   |   |   |   |   |   |
|   |   |   |   |   |   |   |   |   |   |
|   |   |   |   |   |   |   |   |   |   |
|   |   |   |   |   |   |   |   |   |   |
|   |   |   |   |   |   |   |   |   |   |
|   |   |   |   |   |   |   |   |   |   |
|   |   |   |   |   |   |   |   |   |   |
|   |   |   |   |   |   |   |   |   | 100 |

11 Use the digit cards to make 6 different 2-digit numbers.

Write these numbers in the correct places in the 100 square from question 10.

2   4   8

# > 1.2 Counting up to 100 objects

## Exercise 1.2

**Focus**

1  Write the missing numbers.

| | |
|---|---|
| 1 ten → | 10 |
| 2 tens → | |
| 3 tens → | |
| 4 tens → | |
| 5 tens → | |
| 6 tens → | |
| 7 tens → | |
| 8 tens → | |
| 9 tens → | |
| 10 tens → | |

accurate, accurately
collection   order

Use the table to help you count in tens from 10 to 100.

1 Numbers to 100

2 Which tens number is 1 ten more than 8 tens?

3 Which tens number is 1 ten fewer than 6 tens?

4 Sofia and Zara make some numbers. Sofia chooses the tens. Zara chooses the ones.

Write each number they make in a part whole diagram.

a

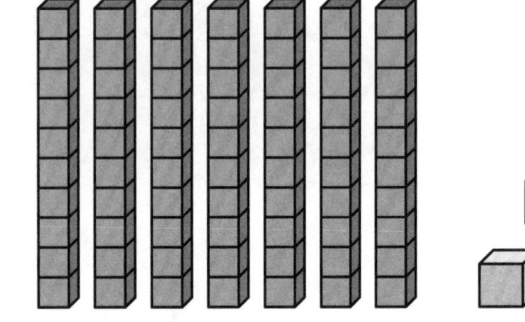

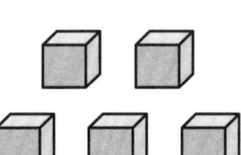

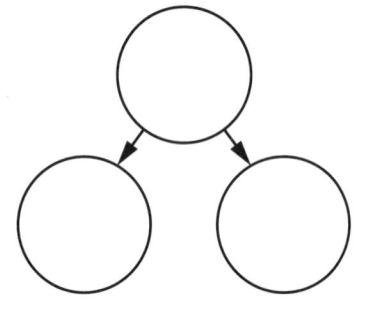

b

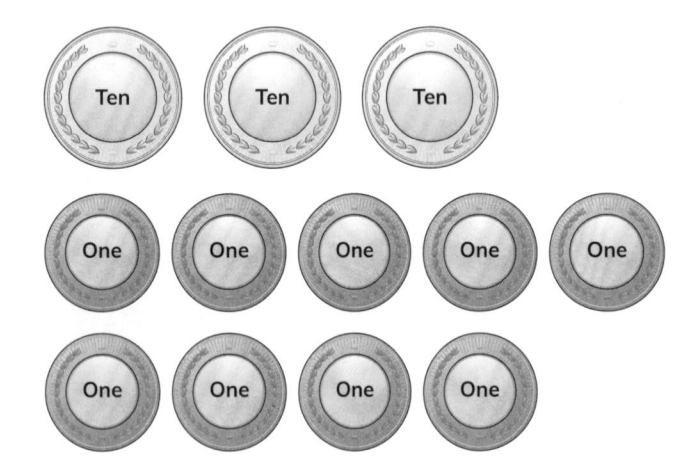

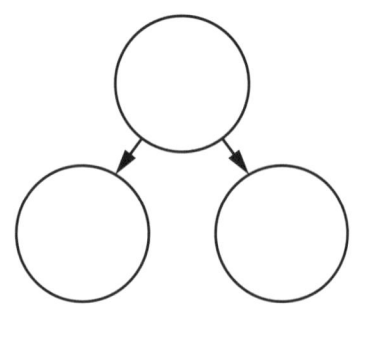

c Sofia chooses four tens.
Zara chooses zero ones.

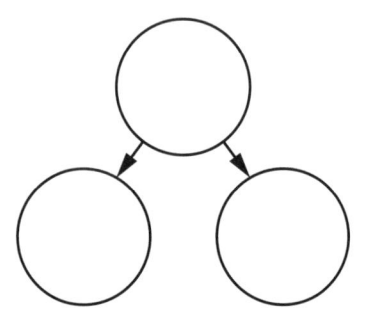

1.2 Counting up to 100 objects

## Worked example 2

Arun scoops some stones out of a tray.
How many stones does he scoop out?
Estimate then count.

> More than 10, but fewer than 50. I estimate 20.

Estimate

10   (20)   50   100

Count

> Count in tens: 10, 20. Count on in ones: 21, 22, 23, 24, 25, 26, 27.

Answer: 27 stones

1 Numbers to 100

5 How many cubes are in the collection?
Estimate then count to check.

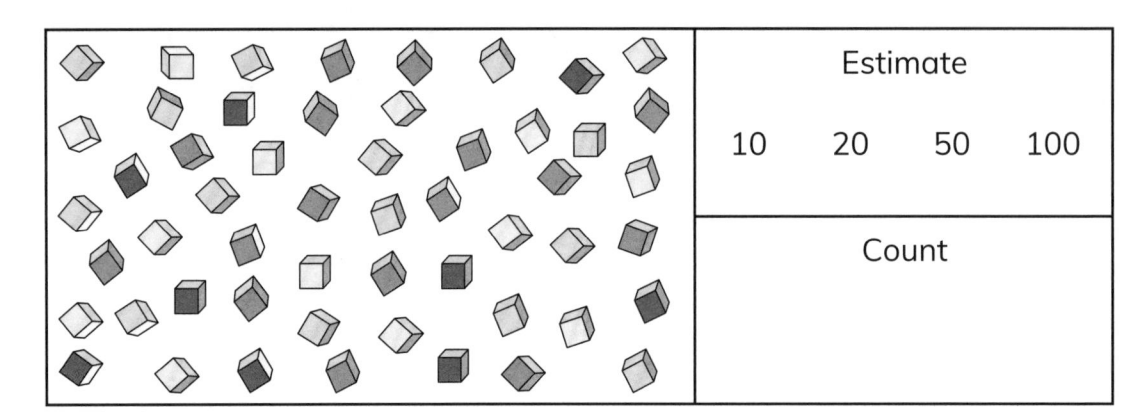

| Estimate | | | |
|---|---|---|---|
| 10 | 20 | 50 | 100 |
| Count | | | |

Compare your estimate and count with another person's.
Do you both agree?

6 Sofia counts 100 beads in twos.

Draw a ring around any numbers she said.

24     59     36     42     17     78     12

## Practice

7 Write the tens numbers in order, from 100 to 10.

| 100 | | | | | | | | | 10 |
|---|---|---|---|---|---|---|---|---|---|

8 Marcus and Arun make some numbers.
Marcus chooses the tens. Arun chooses the ones.

They make 53 and 87.

How many tens does Marcus choose? ☐ and ☐

How many ones does Arun choose? ☐ and ☐

18

9   How many beans are in the collection?

Estimate then count to check.

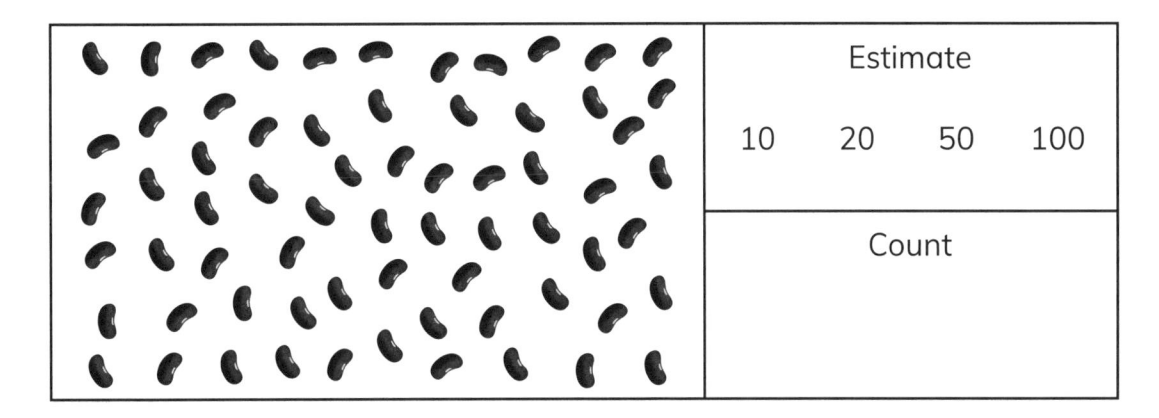

| | Estimate |
|---|---|
| | 10   20   50   100 |
| | Count |

Compare your estimate and count with another person's.
Do you both agree?

10  Tick the correct sentences.

An even number of objects can be sorted into 2 equal groups.

2 more than an odd number is always an odd number.

Numbers with 1, 3, 5, 7 or 9 ones are even numbers.

0 is an odd number.

1 Numbers to 100

## Challenge

11  How many large spots are in the box?

How many small spots are in the box?

Estimate, then use the two boxes below to help you count the large spots and then the small spots.

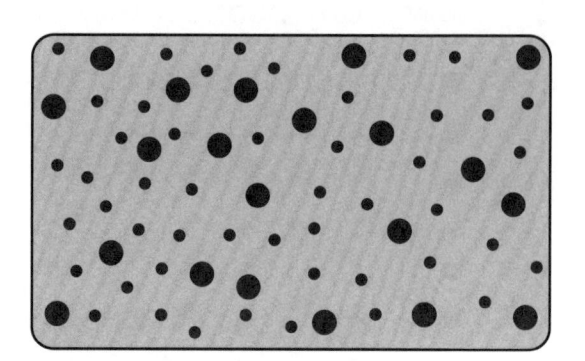

> **Tip**
>
> You could count in twos, fives or tens to find the total.

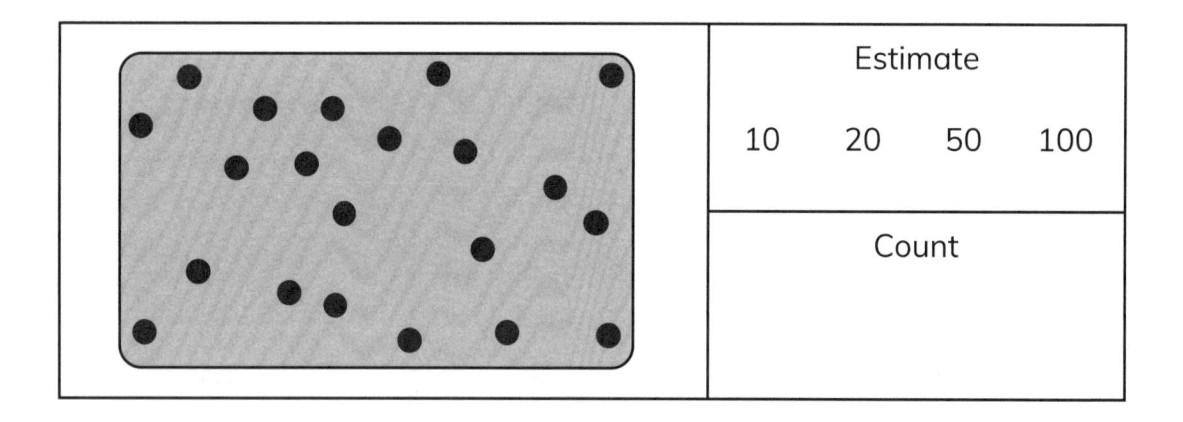

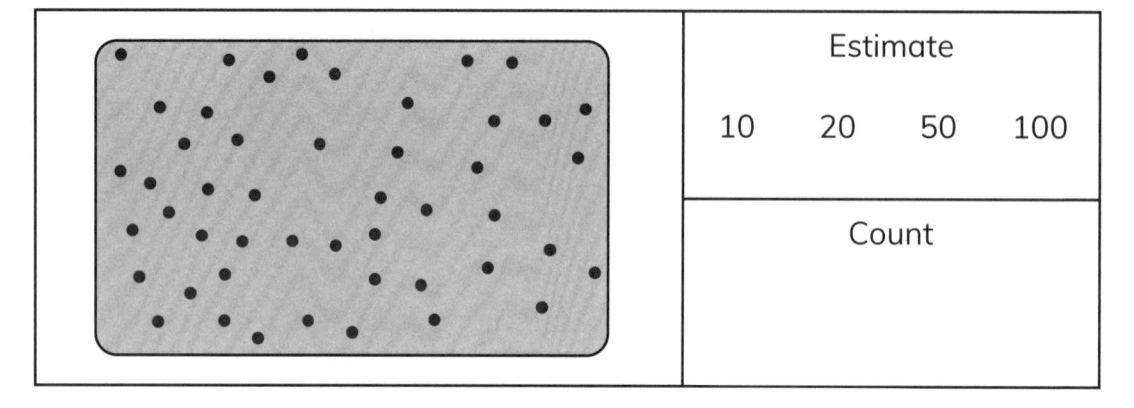

| Estimate |
|---|
| 10   20   50   100 |
| Count |

| Estimate |
|---|
| 10   20   50   100 |
| Count |

Compare your estimate and count with another person's.
Do you both agree?

## 1.2 Counting up to 100 objects

12 Draw or lightly colour a shape joining 5 small squares on the 100 square.

Only 1 number inside your shape can be odd.

| 1 | 2 | 3 | 4 | 5 | 6 | 7 | 8 | 9 | 10 |
|---|---|---|---|---|---|---|---|---|---|
| 11 | 12 | 13 | 14 | 15 | 16 | 17 | 18 | 19 | 20 |
| 21 | 22 | 23 | 24 | 25 | 26 | 27 | 28 | 29 | 30 |
| 31 | 32 | 33 | 34 | 35 | 36 | 37 | 38 | 39 | 40 |
| 41 | 42 | 43 | 44 | 45 | 46 | 47 | 48 | 49 | 50 |
| 51 | 52 | 53 | 54 | 55 | 56 | 57 | 58 | 59 | 60 |
| 61 | 62 | 63 | 64 | 65 | 66 | 67 | 68 | 69 | 70 |
| 71 | 72 | 73 | 74 | 75 | 76 | 77 | 78 | 79 | 80 |
| 81 | 82 | 83 | 84 | 85 | 86 | 87 | 88 | 89 | 90 |
| 91 | 92 | 93 | 94 | 95 | 96 | 97 | 98 | 99 | 100 |

Draw your shape again in a different place.

This time only one of the numbers inside your shape can be even.

# 1 Numbers to 100

## > 1.3 Comparing and ordering numbers

**Exercise 1.3**

**Focus**

> close, closer
> extend a sequence   ordering
> ordinal numbers   sequence

**Worked example 3**

Estimate and show where 32 is on this number line.

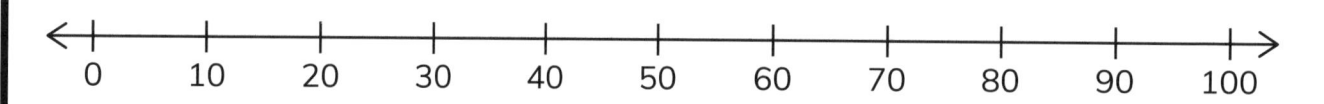

←|———|———|———|———|———|———|———|———|———|———|→
 0   10   20   30   40   50   60   70   80   90  100

**Answer:**

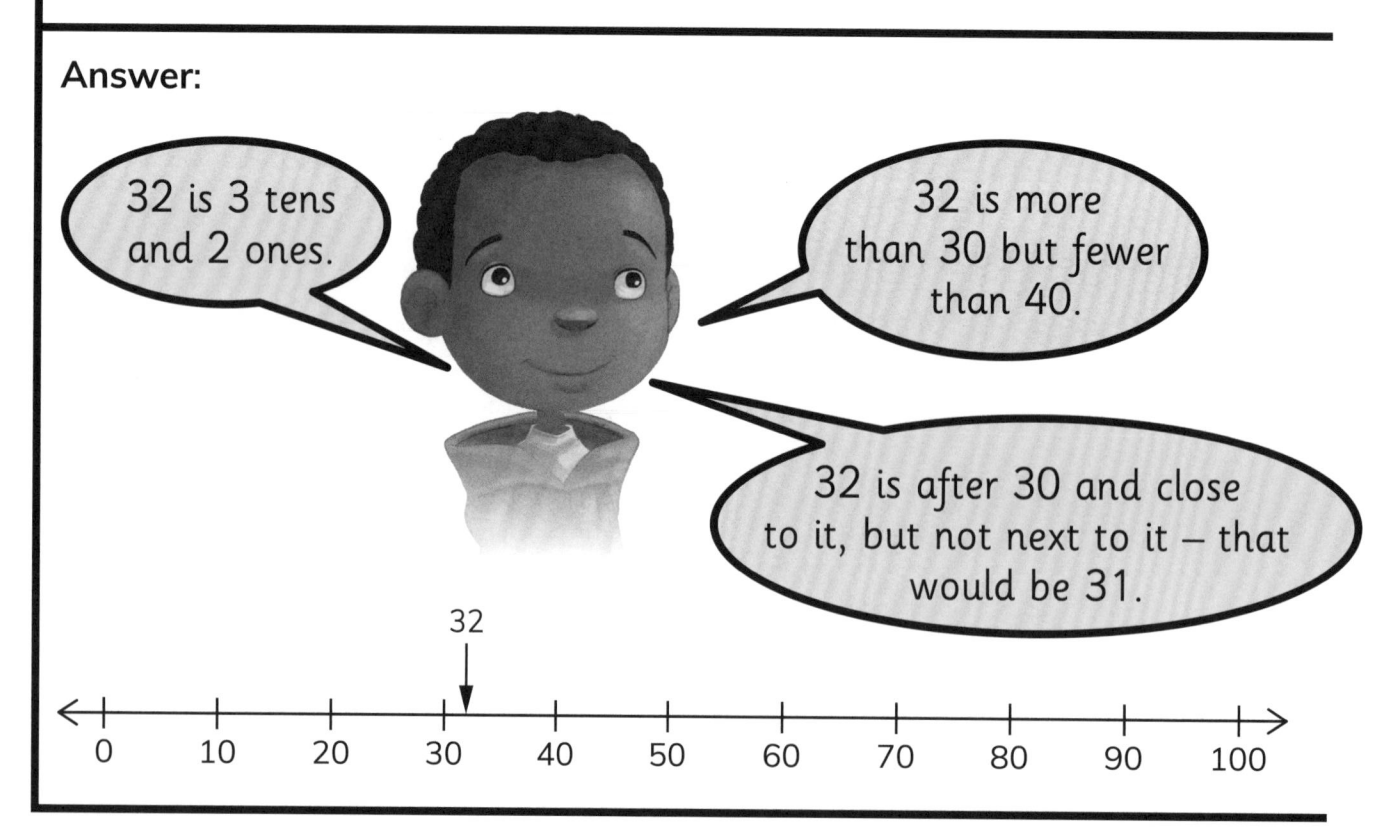

32 is 3 tens and 2 ones.

32 is more than 30 but fewer than 40.

32 is after 30 and close to it, but not next to it — that would be 31.

                    32
                     ↓
←|———|———|———|———|———|———|———|———|———|———|→
 0   10   20   30   40   50   60   70   80   90  100

22 >

1.3 Comparing and ordering numbers

1. Estimate and show where 15, 43 and 78 are on this number line.

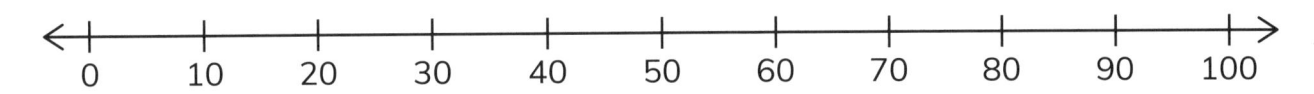

⟵―+―+―+―+―+―+―+―+―+―+―⟶
0  10  20  30  40  50  60  70  80  90  100

2. Draw a ring around the 3rd elephant.

1st

3. Arun is last in a queue of 32 people.

   Write the ordinal number for Arun's place in the queue. ☐

**Worked example 4**

A number sequence starts at 35. It counts on in tens and stops at 65.
What are the numbers in this sequence?

I used a 100 square to help me.

All the numbers have 5 ones. They are all odd.

35, 45, 55, 65.

Answer: 35, 45, 55, 65.

4. A number sequence starts at 42.

   It counts on in tens and stops at 72.

   Write the numbers in the sequence.

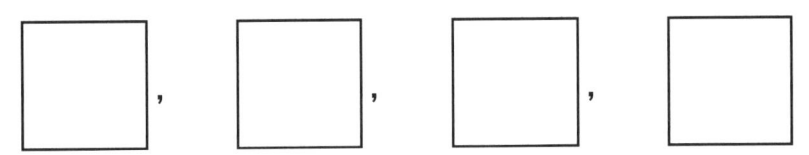

   ☐ , ☐ , ☐ , ☐

## 1 Numbers to 100

5  A number sequence starts at 32.

It counts on in twos and stops at 38.

Write the numbers in the sequence.

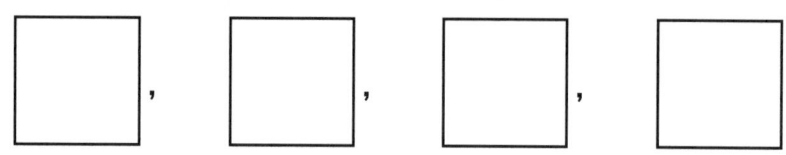

☐ , ☐ , ☐ , ☐

6  Draw a ring around the correct words for the number sequence in question 4.

All the numbers are **odd / even**.

All the numbers have the same number of **ones / tens**.

7  Compare 35 and 53.

Which number is greater? ☐

**Tip**

For questions 7 and 8, you can use the number line or place value grid below to help you.

8  Order these numbers from smallest to greatest.

| 21 |  | 53 |  | 35 |  | 12 |

____  ____  ____  ____

**Tip**

Remember to use a pencil – you can erase your working and reuse the diagrams!

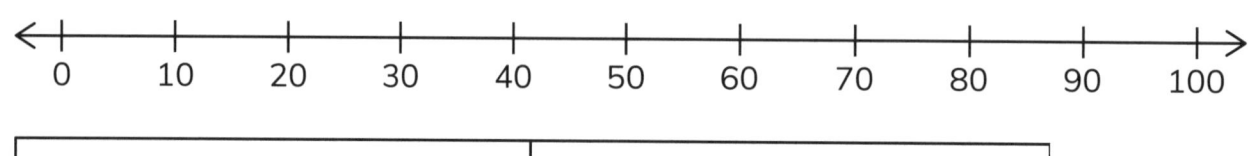

0  10  20  30  40  50  60  70  80  90  100

| 10s | 1s |
|---|---|
|  |  |

24

1.3 Comparing and ordering numbers

## Practice

9  Estimate and show where 3 and 49 are on this number line.

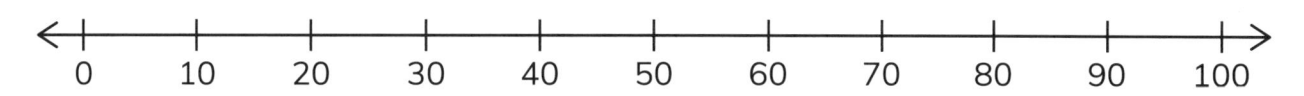

⟵―+―+―+―+―+―+―+―+―+―+―⟶
  0  10  20  30  40  50  60  70  80  90  100

10 Draw a ring around the last leaf.

Draw a line under the 4th leaf.

Tick the 1st leaf.

11 Zara's number sequence is 78, 76, 74, 72, 70.

Complete the description of Zara's number sequence.

_____ at 78. Count _____ in _____. Stop at _____.

12 Compare 63 and 36.
Which is the smaller number?

13 Order these numbers from smallest to largest.

| 64 | 75 | 46 | 57 | 19 |

**Tip**

For questions 12 and 13, you can use the number line or place value grid from questions 7 and 8 to help you.

25

## 1 Numbers to 100

## Challenge

14 Arun marks two numbers on the number line.

Estimate and write Arun's numbers in the boxes.

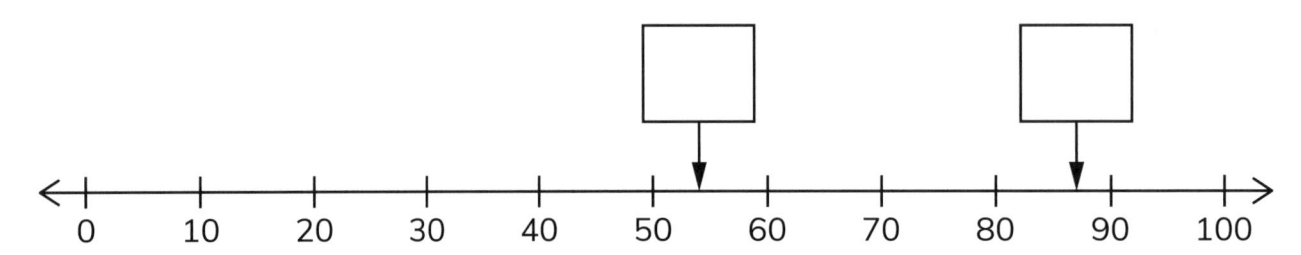

15 Sofia and Zara join a queue to get tickets for the school disco.

There are 51 people in front of them.

What are Sofia and Zara's positions in the queue? _____ and _____

16 Write a sequence of 5 numbers.

Complete the sentences to describe your sequence.

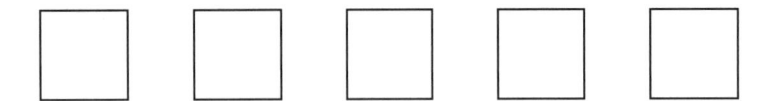

☐ ☐ ☐ ☐ ☐

_____ at _____ . Count _____ in _____ . Stop at _____ .

17 Order these numbers from greatest to smallest.

82  48  84  28  42

_____  _____  _____  _____  _____

# 2 Geometry

> ## 2.1 3D shapes

Exercise 2.1

**Focus**

curved surface   edge
face   vertex, vertices

**Worked example 1**

Match these shapes to their names.

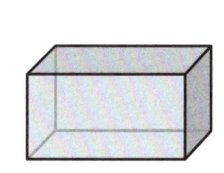

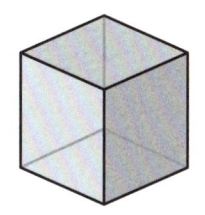

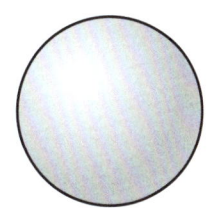

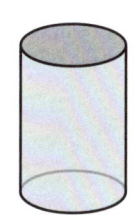

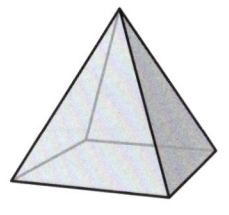

| cube | cuboid | square-based pyramid | cylinder | sphere |

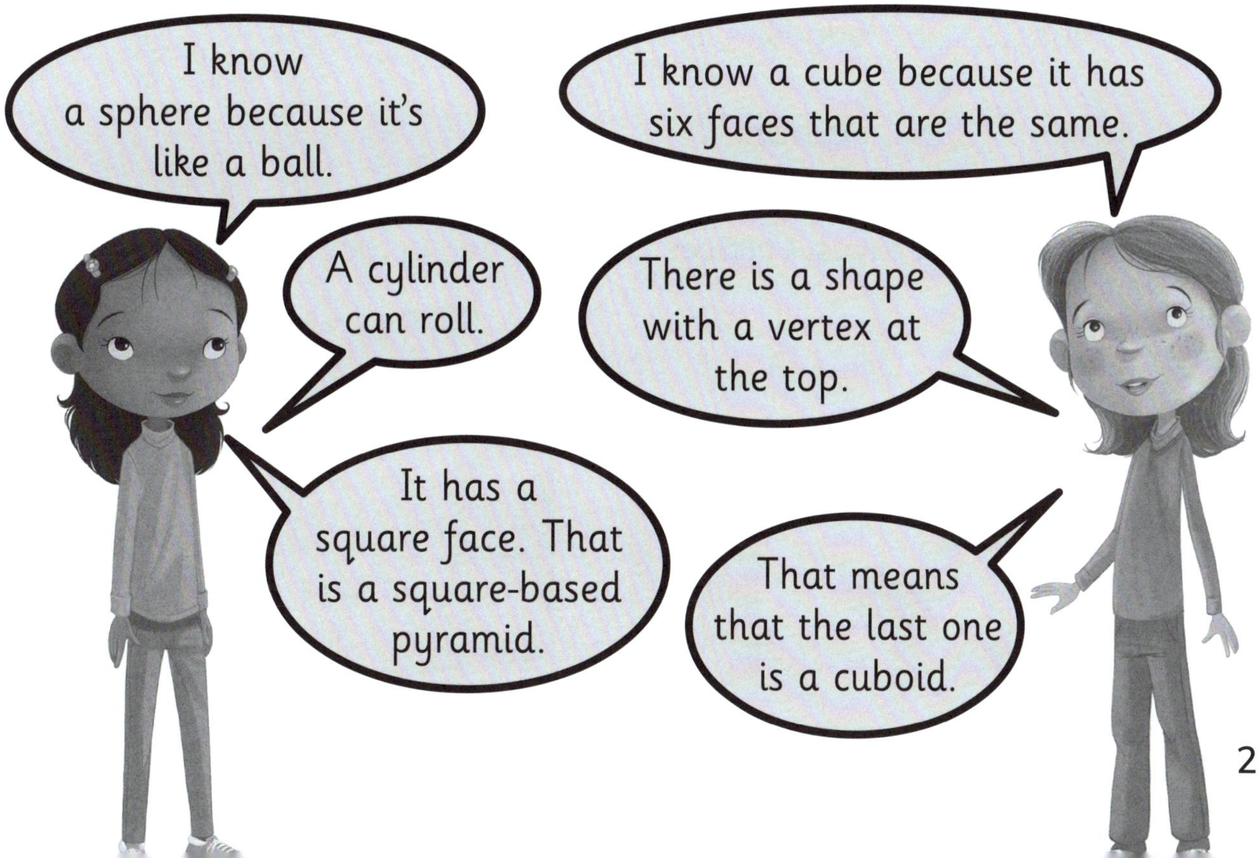

*I know a sphere because it's like a ball.*

*A cylinder can roll.*

*It has a square face. That is a square-based pyramid.*

*I know a cube because it has six faces that are the same.*

*There is a shape with a vertex at the top.*

*That means that the last one is a cuboid.*

27

## 2 Geometry

### Continued

**Answer:**

| cuboid | cube | sphere | cylinder | square-based pyramid |

1  a  Describe this 3D shape.

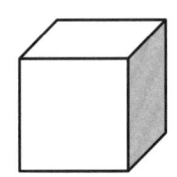

This shape is a _____ .

It has _____ faces.

It has _____ edges.

It has _____ vertices.

b  Choose one of these 3D shapes. Name and describe it using **edges**, **faces**, **vertices** and **curved surfaces**.

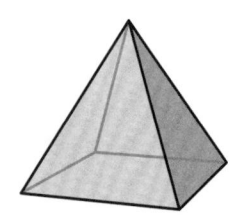

2.1  3D shapes

Name: _____

Description: _____
_____

2   Draw a ring around the correct word to name each shape.

|  | | | | |
|---|---|---|---|---|
|  | sphere | cube | pyramid | cuboid |
|  | cube | cylinder | sphere | cuboid |
|  | sphere | cube | cuboid | cylinder |
|  | cube | cuboid | pyramid | sphere |
|  | cuboid | sphere | pyramid | cube |

29

2 Geometry

3 Look around you.

Find as many 2D and 3D shapes as you can.

Choose 3 of each.

Draw and write what you find in this table.

| Object | Name of 2D shape |
|---|---|
|  |  |
|  |  |
|  |  |

| Object | Name of 3D shape |
|---|---|
|  |  |
|  |  |
|  |  |

## 2.1 3D shapes

4  Complete the number of faces, edges, curved surfaces and vertices in this table.

| Shape | Faces | Edges | Curved surfaces | Vertices |
|---|---|---|---|---|
| sphere | 0 |  |  | 0 |
| cylinder |  |  |  | 0 |
| pyramid | 5 | 8 |  |  |
| cube |  |  |  | 8 |
| cuboid |  | 12 |  |  |

## 2 Geometry

## Practice

5   Tony has a 3D shape.

One face of the shape is a square.

What could the shape be? _____

6   a   What am I? Write the name under the picture.

A

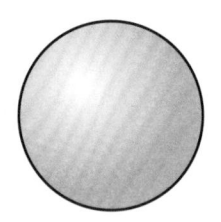

B

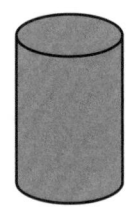

C

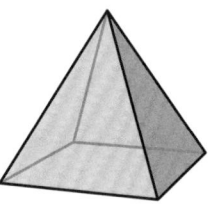

_____    _____    _____

D

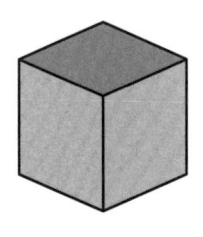

E

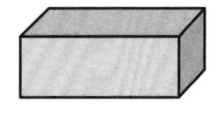

_____    _____

b   I have more than 2 faces.
   None of my faces are circles.
   I have 1 square face.
   Some of my faces are triangles.
   What am I?          I am a _____

c   I have more than 2 vertices.
   I have no triangular faces.
   All my faces are the same size.
   I have no curved surfaces.
   What am I?          I am a _____

7  Use the Venn diagram to sort the shapes.

You can draw the shapes or write their names.

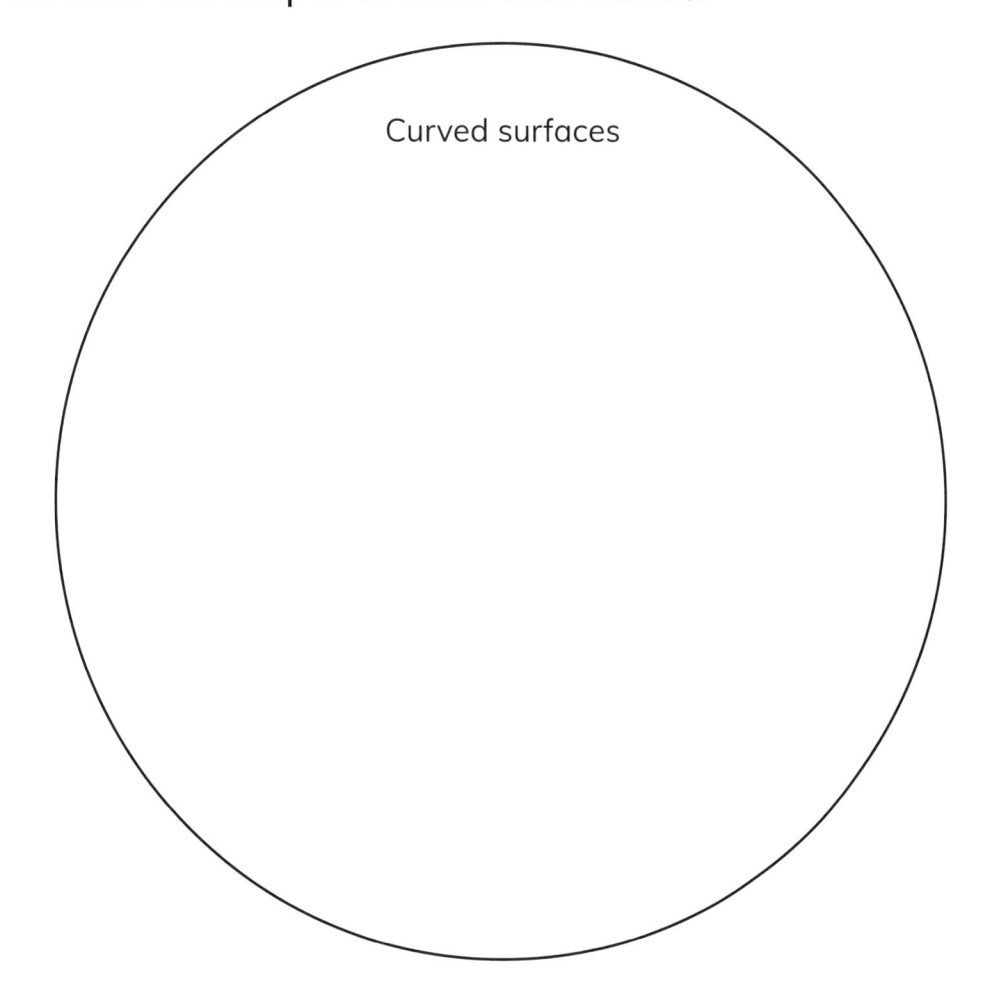

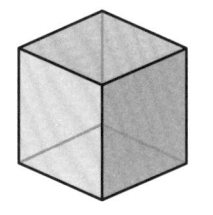

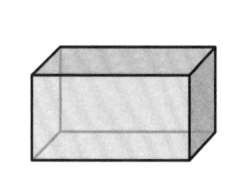

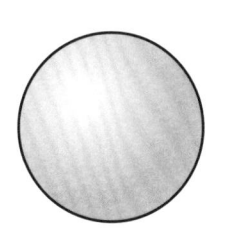

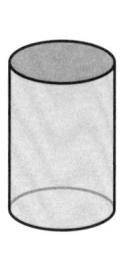

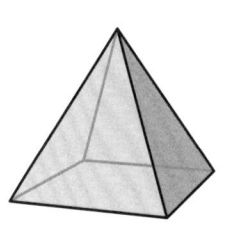

Curved surfaces

## 2 Geometry

8  Find four 3D shapes that are near to you.

What 2D shapes can you find on them?

For example, a cuboid may have 2 square faces and 4 rectangular faces.

Draw and write what you have found in this table.

| Object | Name of 3D shape | 2D shapes you can see |
|---|---|---|
|  |  |  |
|  |  |  |
|  |  |  |
|  |  |  |

## Challenge

9  Susie says that her 3D shape has 12 edges.

Max says that it can be a square-based pyramid, a cube or a cuboid.

Is Max correct? Explain your answer.

_____

_____

10 Look at each pair of shapes.

Can you say what is the same and what is different about the shapes in each pair?

Use the table to record your ideas.

| Shapes | What is the same? | What is different? |
|---|---|---|
| (cube and cuboid) | Both have 6 faces, 12 edges and 8 vertices. | |
| (cylinder and sphere) | | |
| (pyramid and cube) | | |

## 2 Geometry

11  Sort the shapes using a Venn diagram.

Write or draw the shapes in the correct places.

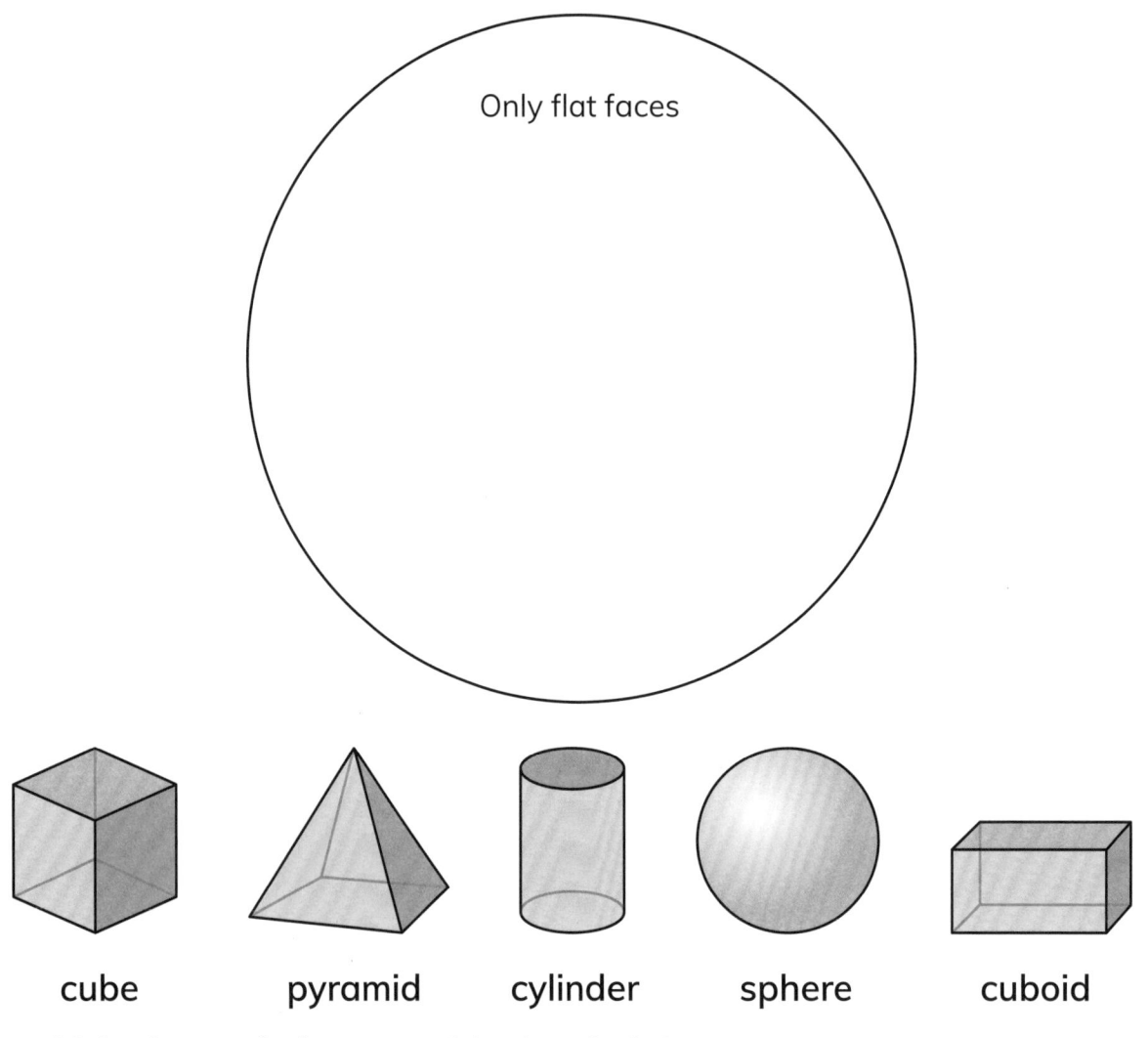

Only flat faces

cube    pyramid    cylinder    sphere    cuboid

Which shapes belong outside the circle?

Write what you notice about the shapes outside the circle.

_____

_____

Which shapes belong inside the circle? Write their names.

_____

2.1 3D shapes

12 Name these 3D shapes.

Then look for and find any of these shapes in or outside your house.

Draw what you find.

Write the name of 2D shapes that can be found on your 3D shapes.

| 3D shape | Name | Picture | 2D shapes I can see |
| --- | --- | --- | --- |
| ⬤ | | | |
| ▢ | | | |
| ▭ | | | |
| ▲ | | | |

37

## 2 Geometry

Name these 2D shapes.

Then look for and find any of these shapes in or outside your home.

Draw what you find.

Write what 3D shapes you can make from your 2D shapes.

| 2D shape | Name | Picture | 3D shapes I can make |
|---|---|---|---|
| ○ | | | |
| □ | | | |
| ▭ | | | |
| △ | | | |

## > 2.2 2D shapes and symmetry

Exercise 2.2

**Focus**

> hexagon   horizontal   line of symmetry
> mirror image   octagon   pentagon
> polygon   symmetry, symmetrical   vertical

**Worked example 2**

Where is the line of symmetry in this shape?

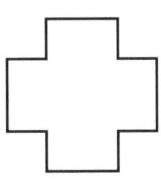

If we fold this shape along the dotted line, the 2 sides will match exactly.

That's called the **line of symmetry**. Some shapes have more than one.

Lots of shapes have a line of symmetry.

1   Draw a line of symmetry on these pictures.

   Use a mirror to help you.

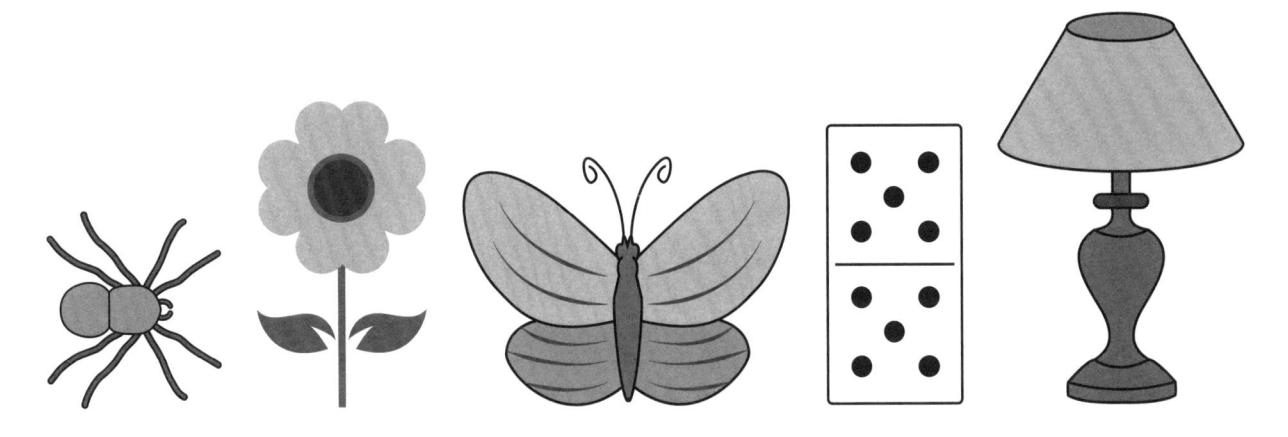

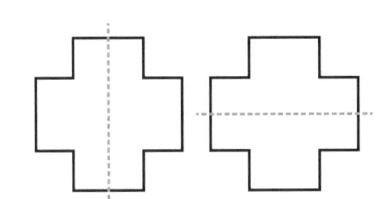

39

## 2 Geometry

**2** Name the shapes. Write sentences to describe the shapes.
Use words like **sides** and **vertices**. Draw any lines of symmetry you can see.

Name: _____

Description: _____

_____

Name: _____

Description: _____

_____

Name: _____

Description: _____

_____

Name: _____

Description: _____

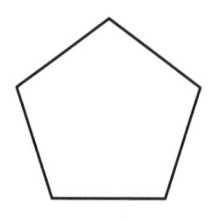

_____

## 2.2 2D shapes and symmetry

**Practice**

3   Tick ✓ the symmetrical pictures.
    Cross ✗ the pictures that are not symmetrical.

    Draw one line of symmetry on the pictures you ticked ✓.

2 Geometry

4 Draw a line to join each shape with the matching symmetrical half.

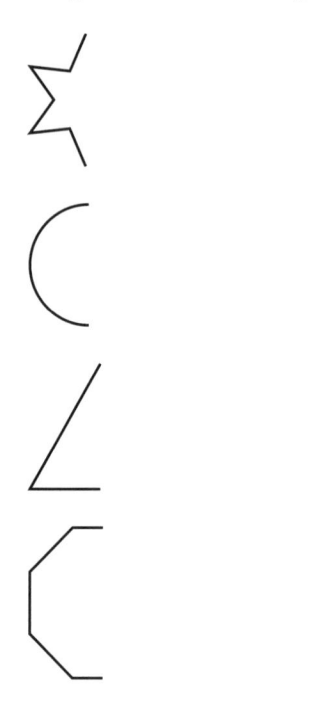

**Challenge**

5 Complete and colour these pictures so that they are symmetrical.

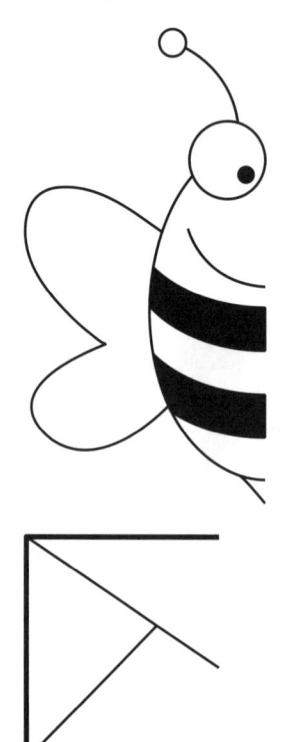

6 Complete the drawing to make it symmetrical.

Colour the completed face.

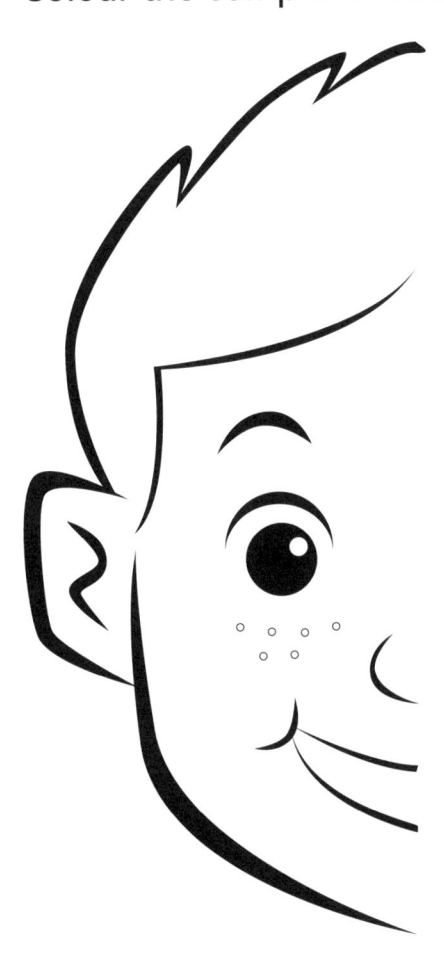

**Tip**

Remember to make the picture symmetrical. You need to think about the colours as well as the shapes.

## 2 Geometry

# > 2.3 Fractions of shapes

Exercise 2.3

**equal parts   fraction   quarter   three-quarters**

**Focus**

> **Worked example 3**
>
> Is each shape divided into halves or quarters?
>
> Draw stripes on one of the halves.
>
> Draw dots on one of the quarters. 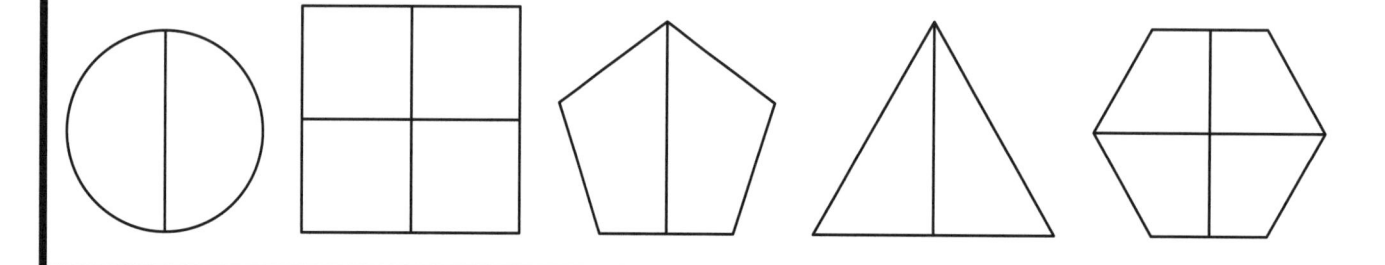
>
> The shapes that have 2 equal parts show halves.
>
> The shapes with 4 equal parts show quarters.
>
> Look at each shape and count the number of equal parts.

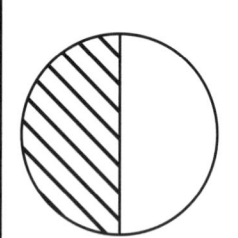

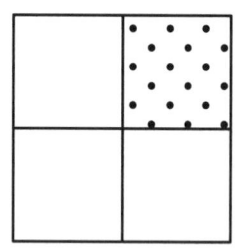

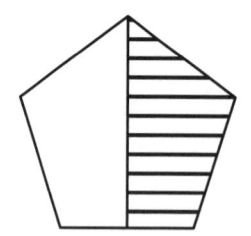

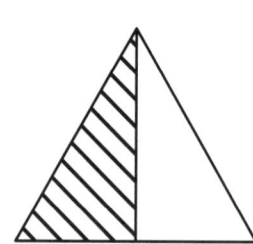

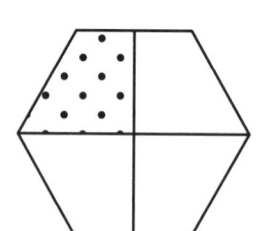

2.3 Fractions of shapes

1  Colour in one half of each shape.

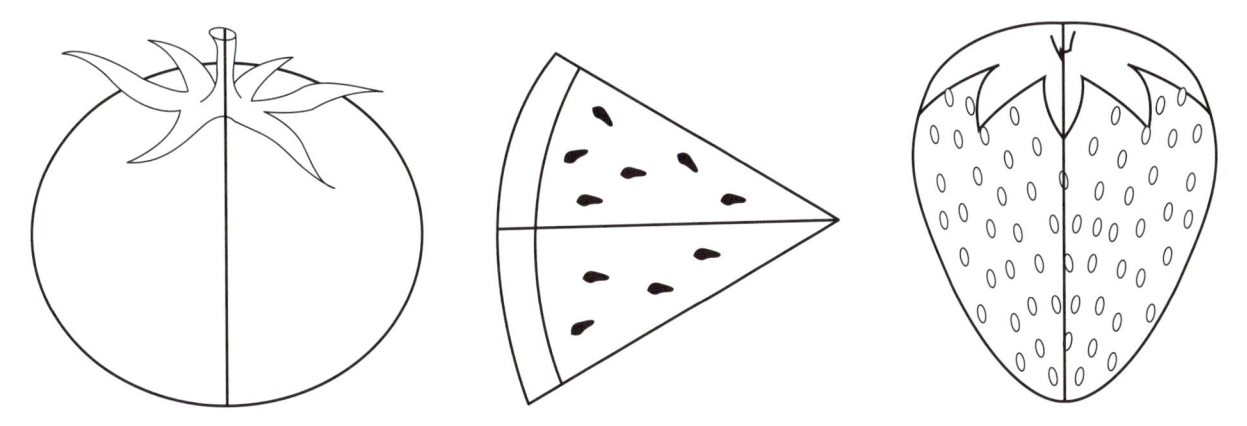

Draw 2 more things you can cut in half.

Colour in one half of each.

## 2 Geometry

2. This shows 2 halves of a square.

   Each part is labelled a $\frac{1}{2}$

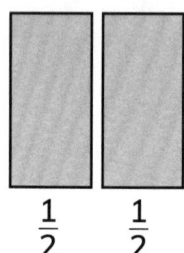

   $\frac{1}{2}$  $\frac{1}{2}$

   $\frac{1}{2} + \frac{1}{2} = 1$ whole

   Find and draw the halves of these shapes and write the number sentence below them.

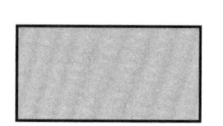

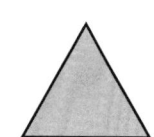

2.3 Fractions of shapes

3   Colour in one quarter of each shape.

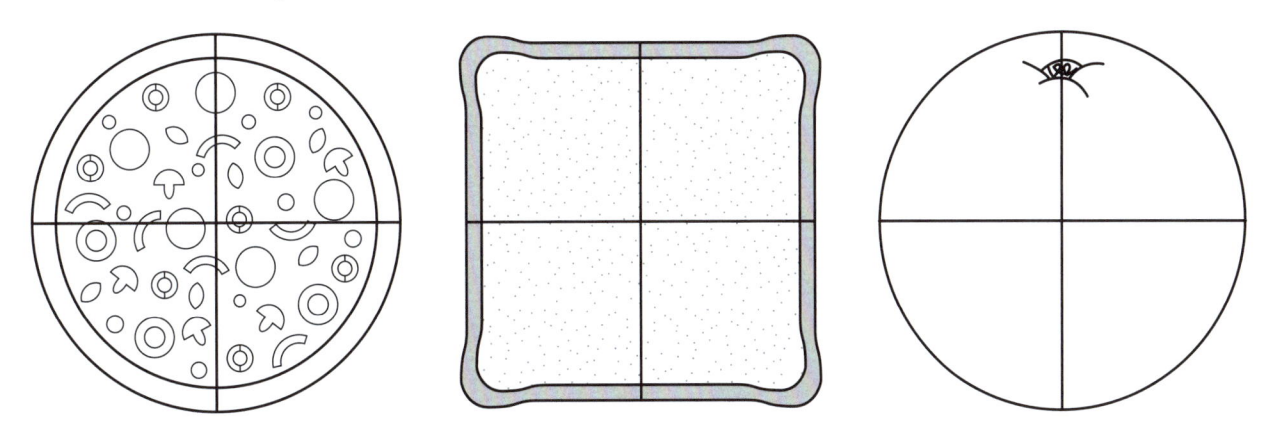

Draw 2 more things you can cut into quarters.

Colour in one quarter of each.

47

## 2 Geometry

**4** Draw 4 shapes of your own and show how to cut them into halves or quarters.

2.3 Fractions of shapes

## Practice

5  Using a colour, complete the shapes to show $\frac{1}{2} + \frac{1}{2} = 1$ whole.

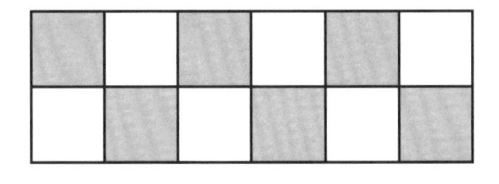

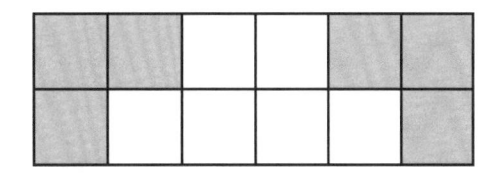

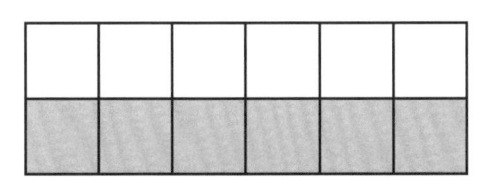

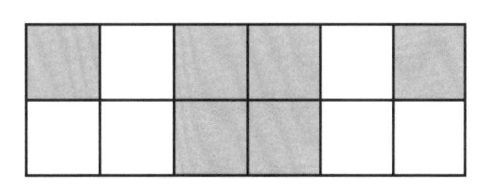

Half of each shape has _____ squares coloured.

Each whole shape has _____ squares coloured.

Complete the number sentence:

$\frac{1}{2}$ + _____ = _____

6  Tick ✓ the shapes that show quarters.

Colour one quarter in each of those shapes.

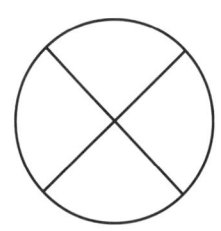

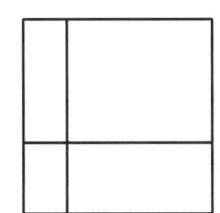

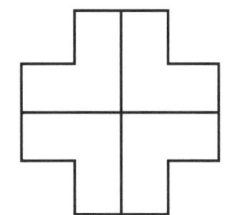

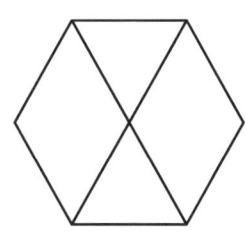

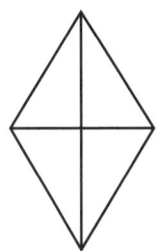

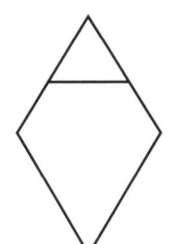

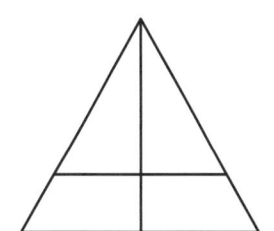

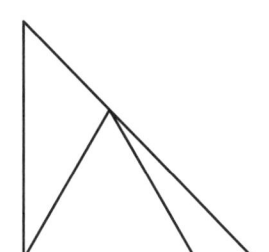

## 2 Geometry

7 Colour a quarter of each shape.

Show a different quarter each time.

## Challenge

8 These biscuits have been broken in half.

How many whole biscuits are there?

Show your working.

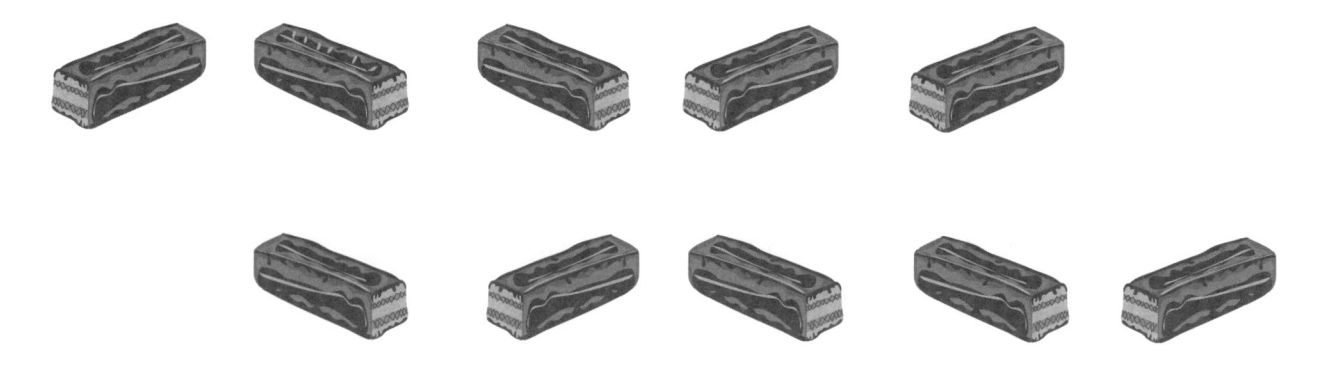

2.3 Fractions of shapes

9  What fraction of each shape has been coloured?

Use $\frac{1}{2}$, $\frac{1}{4}$ and three-quarters for your answers.

a  _____

b  _____

c  _____

10  How many different ways are there to show $\frac{1}{4}$ of a bar of chocolate?

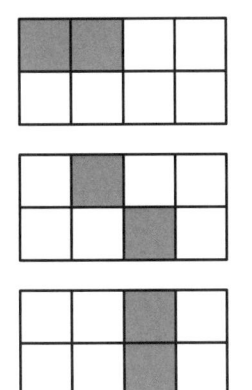

I can find 3 different ways. I'll show you.

Now it's your turn to show 2 more ways.

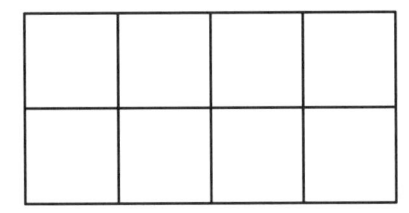

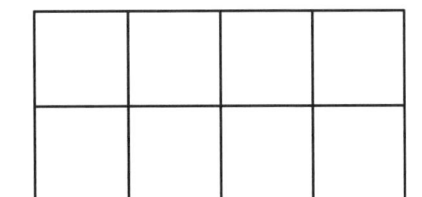

51

## 2 Geometry

**11 a** What fraction of the large square is shaded?

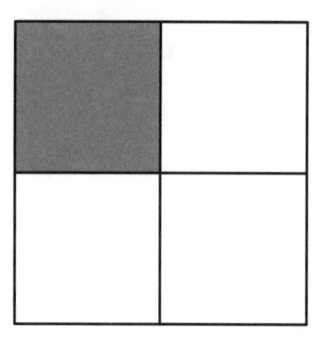

_____

**b** What fraction of the large square is shaded?

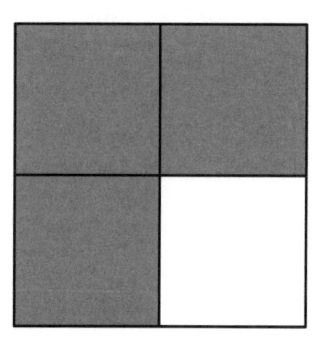

_____

**c** What fraction of the large rectangle is shaded?

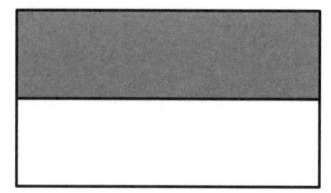

_____

**d** What fraction of the large rectangle has stripes?

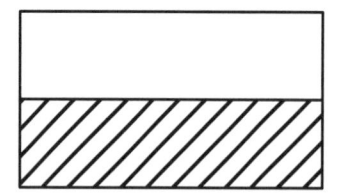

_____

# 3 Measures

## > 3.1 Length

Exercise 3.1

> centimetre  distance  estimate
> height  just over  just under
> length  metre  ruler  width

**Focus**

1   Measure the length of a table using the objects below.

   Record your results.

   | Object | Number |
   |--------|--------|
   | finger |        |
   | hand   |        |
   | pencil |        |
   | spoon  |        |

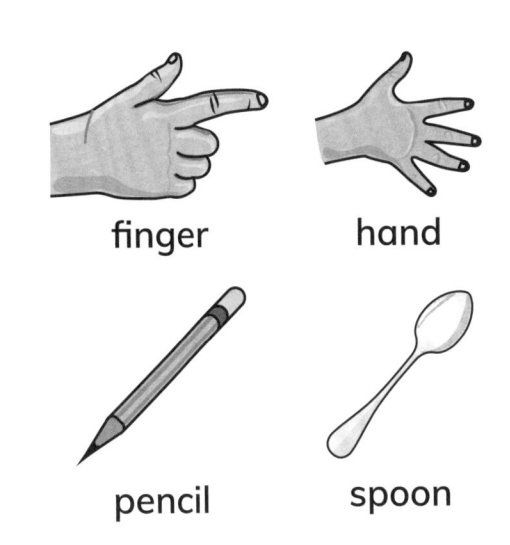

   Are the numbers the same as each other or different?

   Explain the answers.

   _____

   _____

   _____

53

3 Measures

2. Look for objects in the room that are longer or shorter than your shoe.

   Now look for objects in the room that are longer or shorter than a scarf.

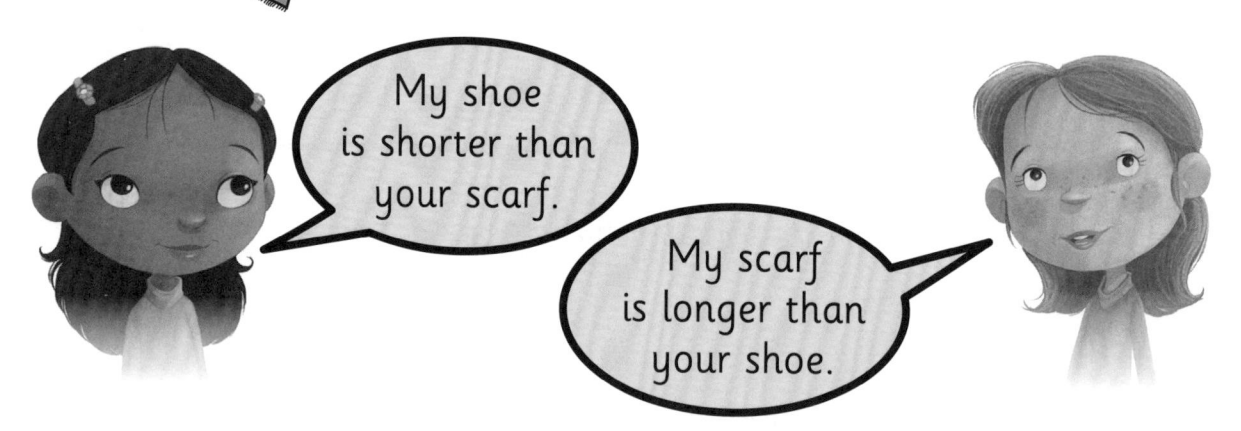

   My shoe is shorter than your scarf.

   My scarf is longer than your shoe.

   Write the name of each object in the table and tick whether they are longer or shorter than the shoe and the scarf.

| Object | Shorter than shoe | Longer than shoe | Shorter than scarf | Longer than scarf |
|---|---|---|---|---|
|  |  |  |  |  |
|  |  |  |  |  |
|  |  |  |  |  |
|  |  |  |  |  |
|  |  |  |  |  |

3.1 Length

3  A ruler is about 30 centimetres long.

Which of these objects are shorter than 30 centimetres, longer than 30 centimetres, or about the same? Estimate your answers.

| Object | Shorter | Longer | About the same |
|---|---|---|---|
| A frying pan | | | |
| A fork | | | |
| Your hand | | | |
| A paint brush | | | |
| Your shoe | | | |
| Your table | | | |
| A skipping rope | | | |
| A straw | | | |

3 Measures

4  Estimate and measure the lengths of these objects.

| Object | Estimate | Measure |
|---|---|---|
|  | ___ centimetres | ___ centimetres |
|  | ___ centimetres | ___ centimetres |
|  | ___ centimetres | ___ centimetres |
|  | ___ centimetres | ___ centimetres |
|  | ___ centimetres | ___ centimetres |
|  | ___ centimetres | ___ centimetres |

**Tip**

Use your ruler when you **measure**. Do not use your ruler when you **estimate**.

3.1 Length

## Practice

5   Use these objects to measure the length of your arm and your leg.

Write your answers in the table.

| How long is your arm? | How long is your leg? |
|---|---|
| _____ fingers | _____ fingers |
| _____ hands | _____ hands |
| _____ pencils | _____ pencils |
| _____ spoons | _____ spoons |

Explain why the answers are different.

_____

_____

## 3 Measures

**6** Use a ruler. Measure and write the length of this pen.

_____ centimetres

Draw something that is longer than the pen. How long is it?

Draw something that is shorter than the pen. How long is it?

3.1 Length

7. Would you measure these things using centimetres or metres?

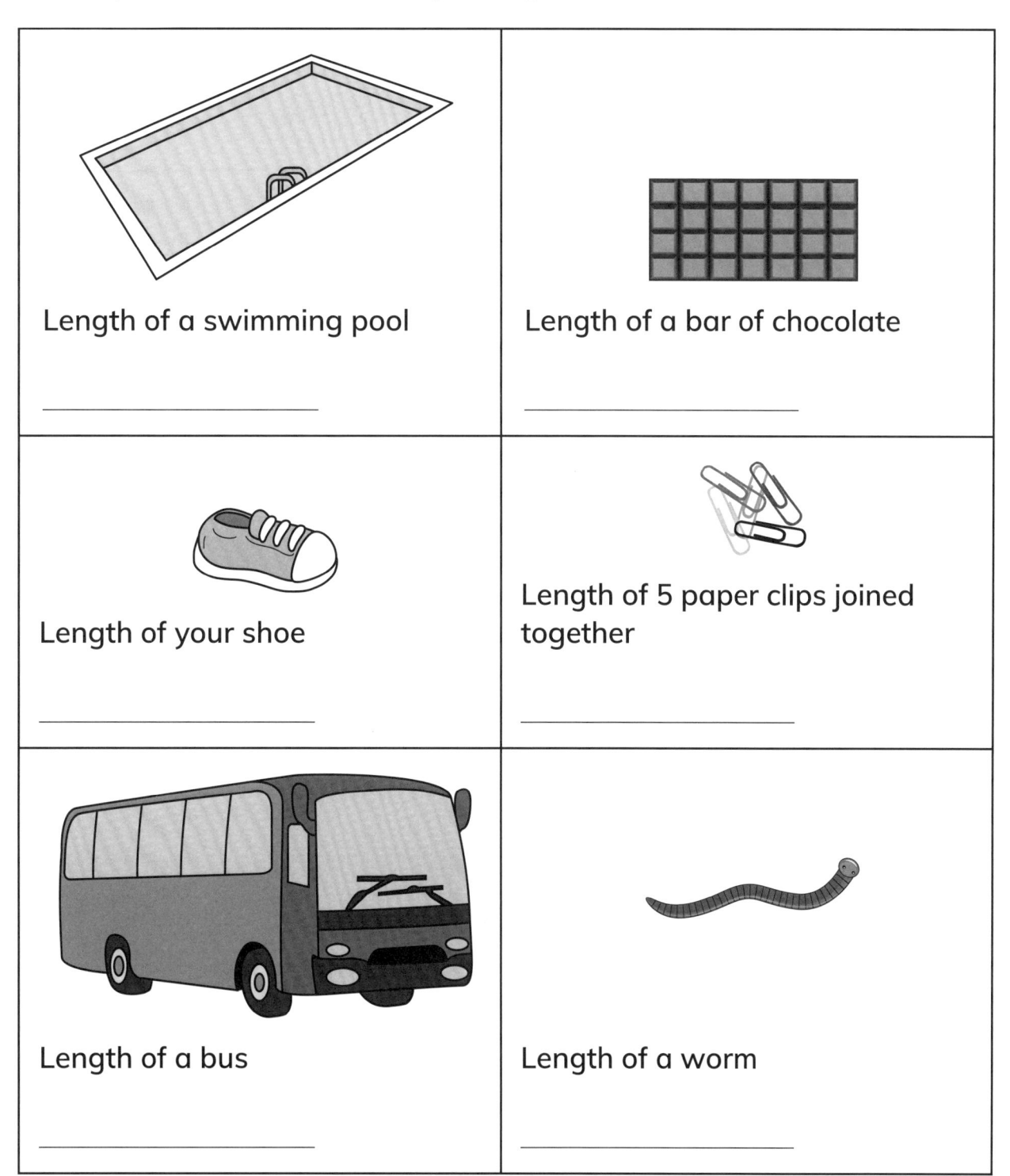

| | |
|---|---|
| Length of a swimming pool | Length of a bar of chocolate |
| Length of your shoe | Length of 5 paper clips joined together |
| Length of a bus | Length of a worm |

## 3 Measures

8 Write and draw five things you can see that are about 15 centimetres long.

3.1 Length

## Challenge

9   Look around your home.

Without using a tape measure, what could you use to measure how long a pencil is? What could you use to measure the length of your bedroom?

Draw and write what you used and what you found out.

10  Estimate and then measure the length of each bar. The rulers are marked in centimetres.

**Tip**

Look where the bars start.

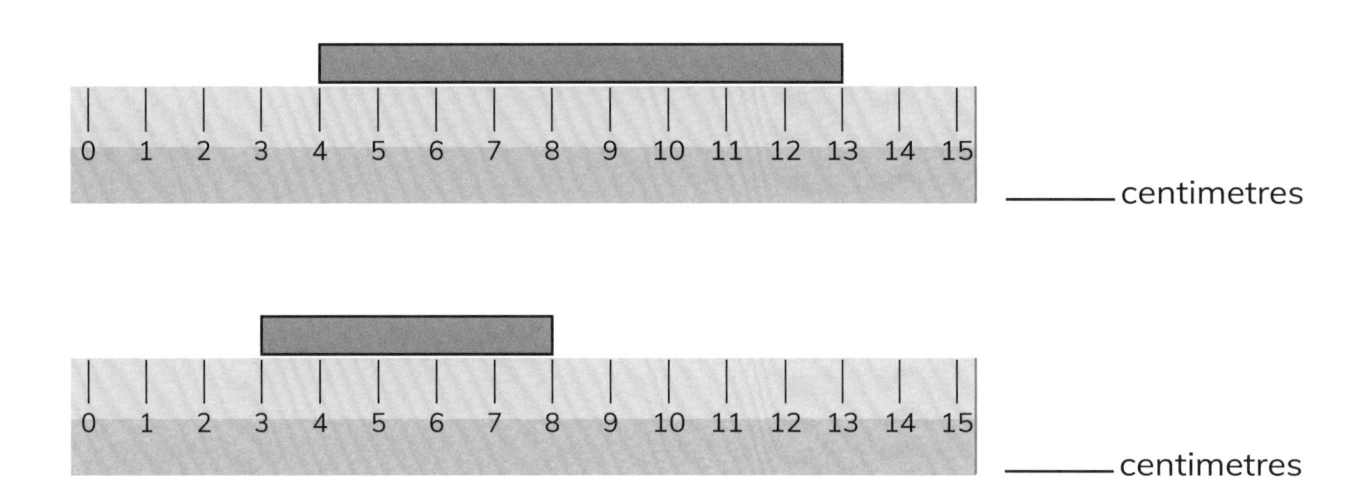

_____ centimetres

_____ centimetres

3 Measures

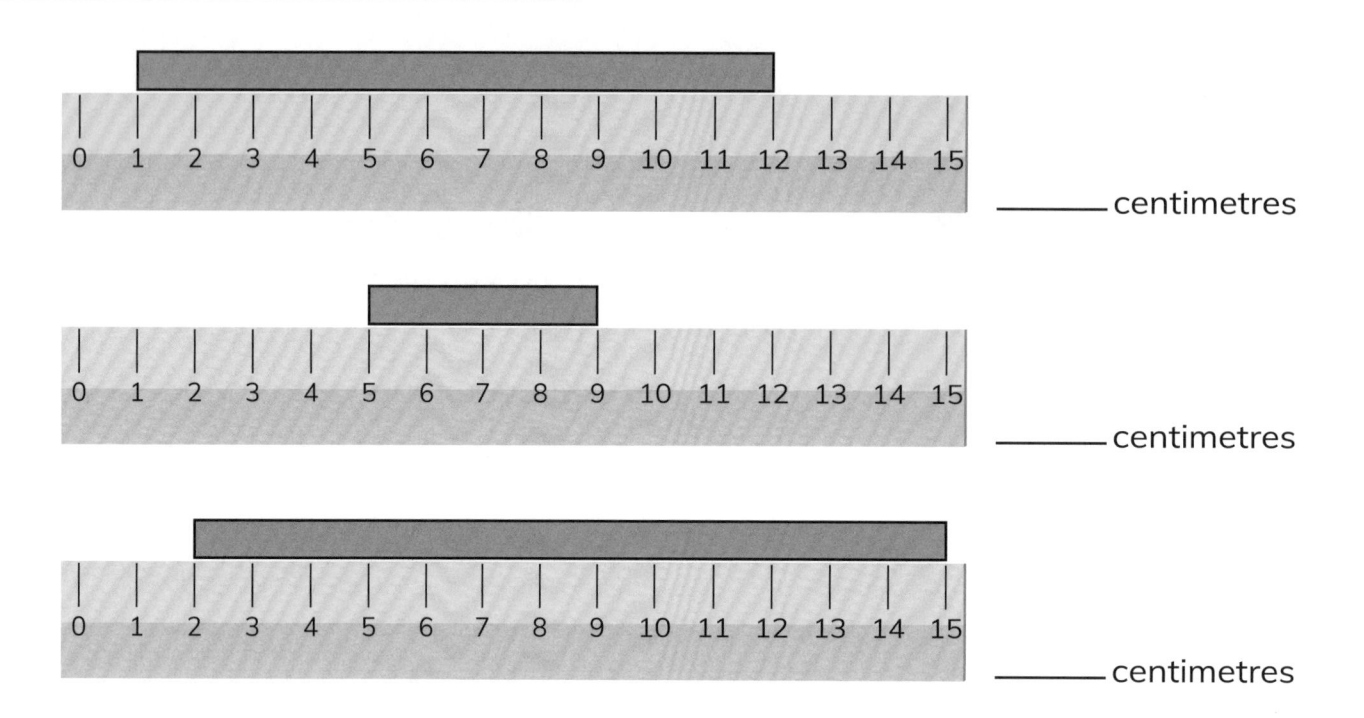

_____ centimetres

_____ centimetres

_____ centimetres

11 Write these lengths in order, starting with the shortest.

a   30 centimetres   70 centimetres   50 centimetres   39 centimetres

_____

_____

b   77 centimetres   88 centimetres   78 centimetres   87 centimetres

_____

_____

c   1 metre   3 metres   4 metres   $\frac{1}{2}$ metre

_____

_____

12 Estimate how far you can jump.

Show where you will start and where you will land, then measure the distance.

From your starting line, put your feet together, swing your arms and jump. Measure the actual distance you jumped.

How close was your estimate? Have another go.
Is your estimate any closer?

| Estimate | Actual distance |
|---|---|
| centimetres | centimetres |
| centimetres | centimetres |

# 3 Measures

## > 3.2 Drawing and measuring lines

### Exercise 3.2

**Focus**

1. Use a ruler to measure the length of each line.

    > **Tip**
    >
    > Remember to put 0 or the end of your ruler at the beginning of the line.

    a _____

    _____ centimetres

    b ____

    _____ centimetres

    c _____

    _____ centimetres

    d _____

    _____ centimetres

    e _____

    _____ centimetres

3.2 Drawing and measuring lines

2   You will need a ruler to measure how long or how wide these things are.

My hand is about _____ centimetres wide.

My arm is about _____ centimetres long.

My arm span is about _____ centimetres long.

My hand is about _____ centimetres long.

My longest finger is about _____ centimetres long.

Across my foot is about _____ centimetres wide.

What was difficult to measure with a ruler?

_____

What would you use next time?

_____

How many centimetres long was the longest thing you measured? _____

How many centimetres wide was the shortest thing you measured? _____

### Tip

The length of an object is usually longer than the width.

Use a tape measure or put rulers end to end to measure longer objects.

65

## 3 Measures

**Practice**

3   Use a tape measure to measure:

a   the length of your room.
Use words such as metre, centimetre, just over, just under.

_____

_____

b   the width of your room.
Use words such as metre, centimetre, just over, just under.

_____

_____

4   Find other lengths at school or at home that you can safely measure using a tape measure.

| Draw or write what you are measuring | Measurement |
|---|---|
|  | metres |
|  | metres |
|  | metres |
|  | metres |

3.2 Drawing and measuring lines

5   a   Choose whether you would use metres or centimetres
        to measure the lengths of these objects.

    Draw a ring around **metres** or **centimetres**.

| a pencil case | metres | centimetres |
| a bus | metres | centimetres |
| a pencil | metres | centimetres |
| a wall | metres | centimetres |
| a book | metres | centimetres |
| a car | metres | centimetres |

   b   Draw or write 4 more things you would measure using metres.

Draw or write 4 more things you would measure using centimetres.

67

## 3 Measures

## Challenge

6   Explore measuring in centimetres. Which line is longer?

A ─────────────────────────────
B ───────────────────────────

How much longer is the line? _____

7   Which line is shorter?

A ──────────────────────
B ────────────────────────────

How much shorter is the line? _____

8   Which line is shorter?

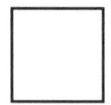

A ──────────────
B ──────

How much shorter is the line?

_____

**Tip**

Remember to put 0 or the end of your ruler at the beginning of the line.

3.2 Drawing and measuring lines

9   Which line is longer?

A ─────────────────────────────

B ─────────────────────────────

☐

How long is the longest line? _____

How long is the shortest line? _____

How much longer is the longest line? _____

Use your ruler to find out.

10  These rulers are marked in centimetres.

Choose one answer. Draw a ring around the one you choose.

a

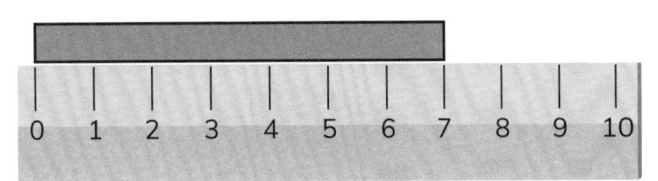

The shaded rectangle is:   6 centimetres   7 centimetres   long.

b   How long is the striped rectangle? _____

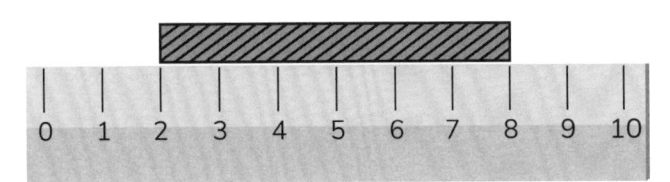

c   How long is the spotty rectangle? _____

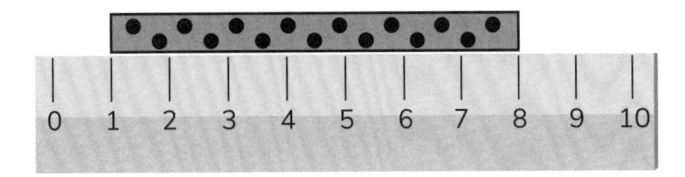

69

## 3 Measures

**11** Draw a ring around the correct answer.

> **Tip**
>
> You do not need to measure the pictures on the page for this question.

a   The height of an apple is about:

   3 centimetres     60 centimetres     10 centimetres     1 metre

b   The height of a strawberry is about:

   25 centimetres     5 centimetres     1 metre     15 centimetres

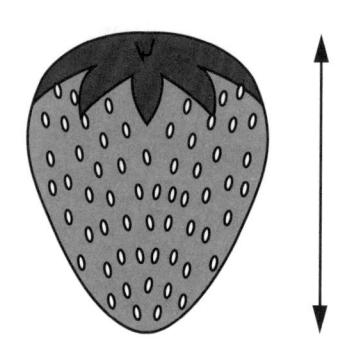

c   The length of a pencil is about:

   1 metre     120 centimetres     20 centimetres

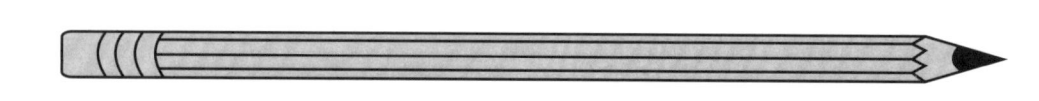

3.2 Drawing and measuring lines

d   The height of a tree is about:

   100 centimetres     30 centimetres     5 metres

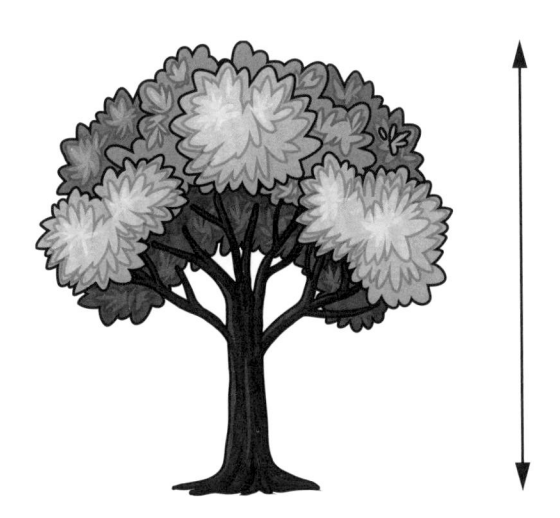

e   The length of a plaster is about:

   55 centimetres     5 centimetres     1 metre

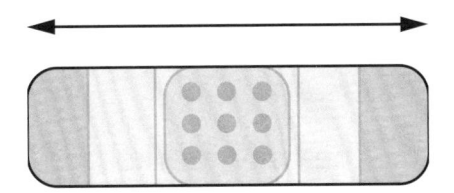

71

# 4 Statistics

## > 4.1 Carroll diagrams and tally charts

Exercise 4.1

**Focus**

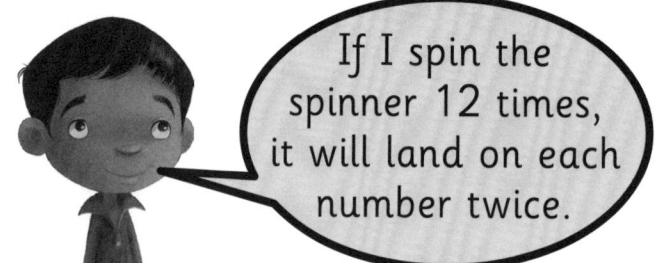

> Carroll diagram
> least popular
> most popular
> non-statistical question
> statistical question
> tally   tally chart

1   *If I spin the spinner 12 times, it will land on each number twice.*

Do you think Arun is correct? How could you check?

Using a pencil, hold a paper clip at the centre of the spinner. Spin the paper clip and draw the dice face it lands on.

Spin the spinner 12 times. Draw a tally mark for each dice face that it lands on.

After 12 spins, count up the tally marks and write the numbers.

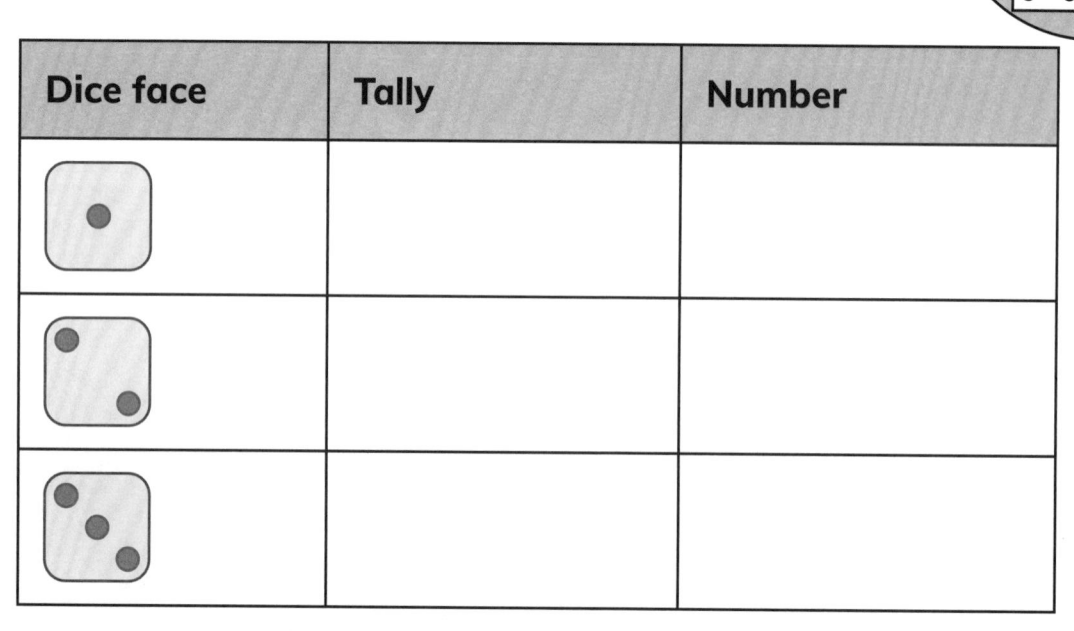

| Dice face | Tally | Number |
|---|---|---|
| ⚀ | | |
| ⚁ | | |
| ⚂ | | |

| Dice face | Tally | Number |
|---|---|---|
| ⚃ | | |
| ⚄ | | |
| ⚅ | | |

What did your experiment show you? Was Arun correct?

2   Draw the shapes to complete the Carroll diagram.

|  | Triangle | Not triangle |
|---|---|---|
| Striped | | |
| Not striped | | |

## 4 Statistics

## Practice

3 Count the starfish.

Use tally marks to show how many starfish are in each group.

Write the total.

| Starfish | Tally | Number |
|---|---|---|
| (6 starfish) | ⊁⊁⊁⊁⊁ I | 6 |
| (12 starfish) | | |
| (9 starfish) | | |
| (5 starfish) | | |
| (14 starfish) | | |
| (4 starfish) | | |
| (15 starfish) | | |

4.1 Carroll diagrams and tally charts

4  This tally chart shows the number of bikes a shop sold in 4 weeks.

| Bikes sold in a week | Tally |
|---|---|
| Week 1 | ||||  ||||  ||||  | |
| Week 2 | ||||  ||||  ||||  |||| |
| Week 3 | ||||  ||||  ||||  ||||  || |
| Week 4 | ||||  ||||  ||||  ||||  ||||  |||| |

How many bikes are sold in the 4th week? _____

How many bikes are sold in the 1st week? _____

How many bikes are sold altogether in the 2nd and 3rd weeks? _____

How many bikes are sold in the 4 weeks altogether? _____

5  Sort the shapes in the Carroll diagram using arrows. The first one has been done for you.

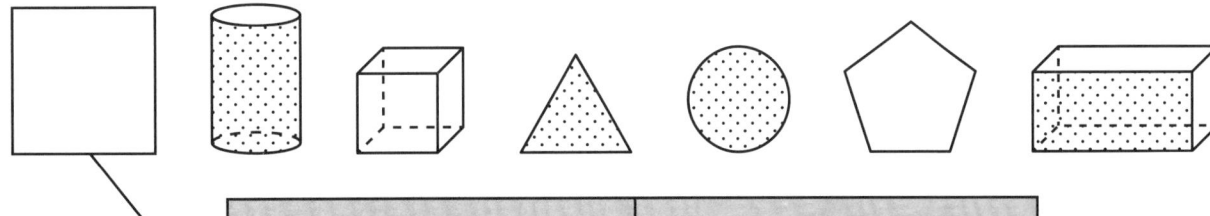

|  | 2D shape | Not a 2D shape |
|---|---|---|
| Spots |  |  |
| No spots |  |  |

## 4 Statistics

**Challenge**

6. Using a pencil, hold a paper clip at the centre of the circle.

   Spin the paper clip.
   Where does it stop on the spinner?

   Have 12 spins altogether.

   Record your results in the tally chart.

| Animal | Tally marks | Number |
|---|---|---|
| lion | | |
| tiger | | |
| giraffe | | |
| horse | | |
| monkey | | |

Play the game again.
Write the results in a different colour in the tally chart.

Discuss your results with a parent or carer. Are the results the same for both games?
What is the same and what is different?
Why do you think this happened?

7 Sort the animals by writing the names in the correct areas in the Carroll diagram.

dolphin

penguin

eagle

tiger

hen

tortoise

fish

bee

snake

|  | Can fly | Cannot fly |
|---|---|---|
| 2 or fewer legs | | |
| Not 2 or fewer legs | | |

Now, choose 1 different animal to add to each box.

# 5 Working with numbers to 100

## > 5.1 Addition

Exercise 5.1

> column addition   complement (of 10, 20 and tens numbers to 100)   digit   place holder   place value grid

**Focus**

1   How many counters are there?

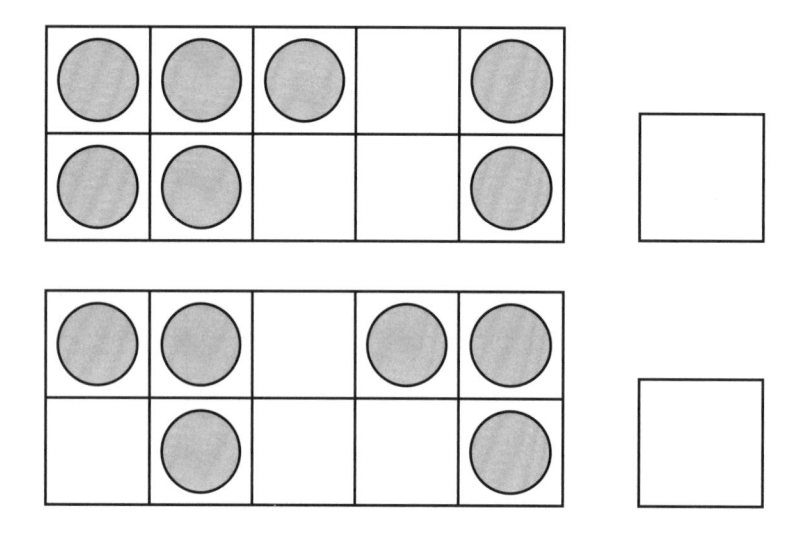

   Talk to your partner or carer about what you see. Ask them what they see.

2   Draw two different arrangements for 5 on the ten frames.

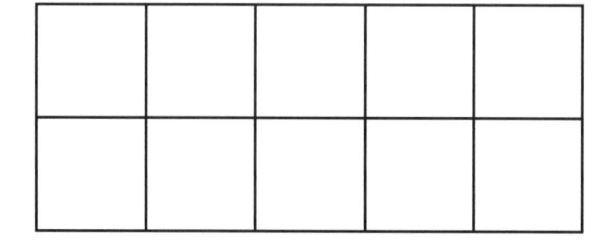

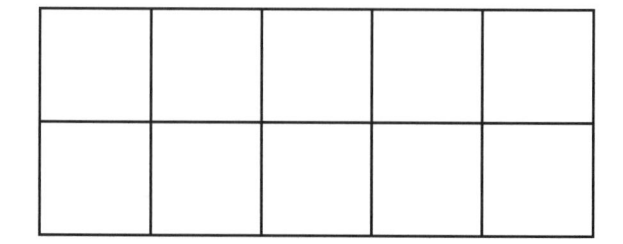

5.1 Addition

**Worked example 1**

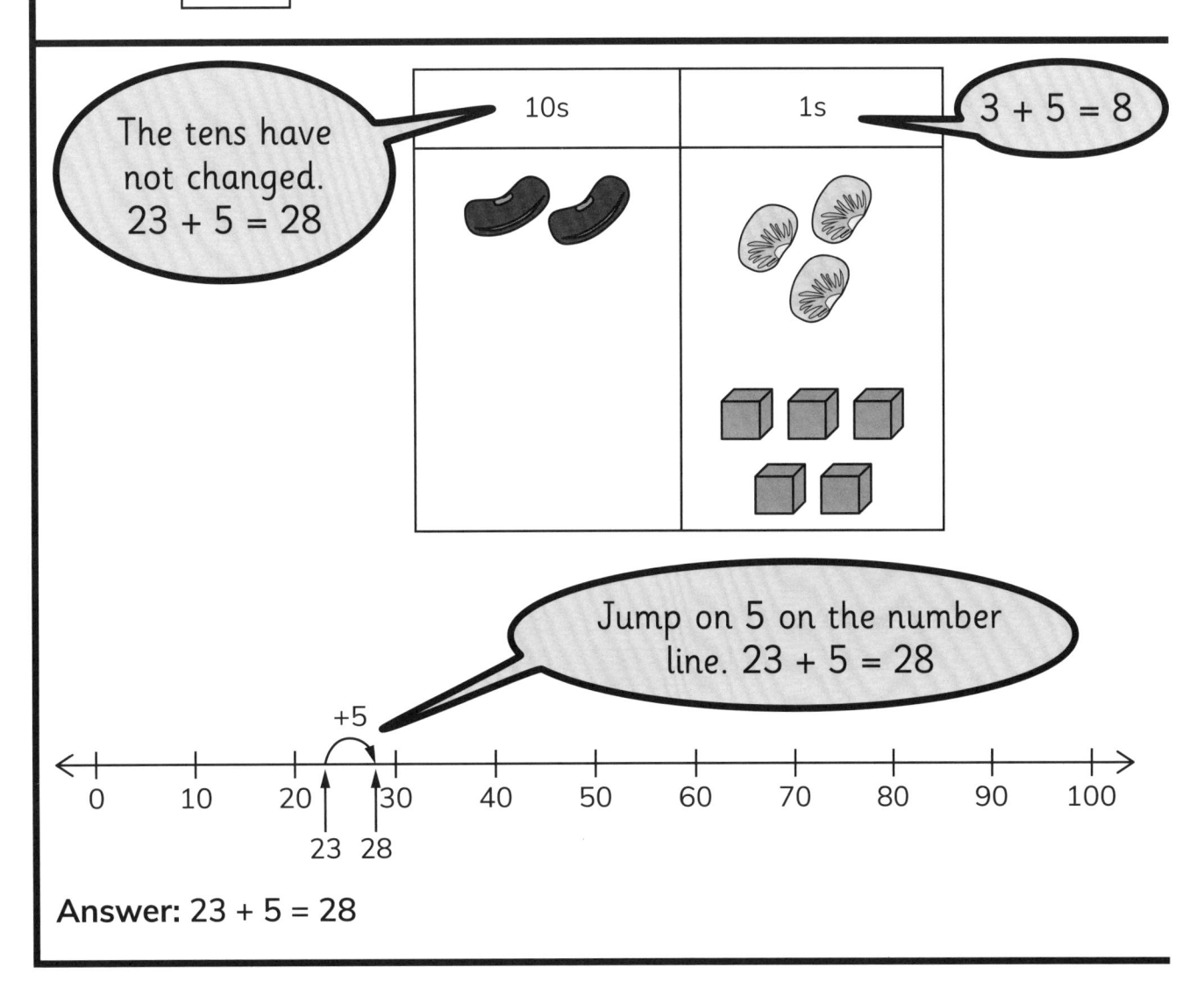

23 + 5 = ☐

*The tens have not changed. 23 + 5 = 28*

| 10s | 1s |

*3 + 5 = 8*

*Jump on 5 on the number line. 23 + 5 = 28*

+5
0  10  20  23  28  30  40  50  60  70  80  90  100

**Answer:** 23 + 5 = 28

3  Find the totals. You can use the number line in question 4 to help you.

a  25 + 4 = ☐

b  42 + 5 = ☐

c  51 + 7 = ☐

d  33 + 6 = ☐

5 Working with numbers to 100

4 Find the totals. You can use the number line to help you.

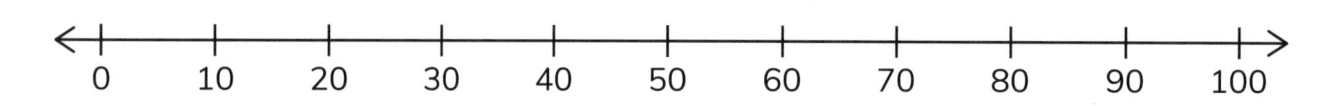

0  10  20  30  40  50  60  70  80  90  100

a  28 + 10 = ☐

b  32 + 10 = ☐

c  54 + 20 = ☐

d  41 + 20 = ☐

5 Complete the calculation.

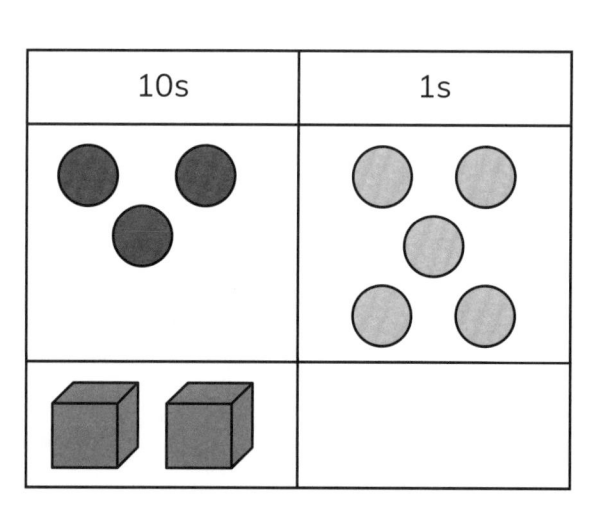

|     | 10s | 1s |
|-----|-----|----|

```
    3   5
+  ☐   ☐
   ─────
   ☐   ☐
```

5.1 Addition

6   Find the total of each set of three numbers.

   a   5 + 5 + 5 = ☐          b   6 + 5 + 4 = ☐

   c   8 + 4 + 2 = ☐

   Did you add the numbers in the same order as they are written or did you do something else?

   Discuss different ways to find the totals with a partner or carer.

## Practice

7   Find the totals.

   a   64 + 5 = ☐            b   31 + 8 = ☐

   c      84                  d      92
       +   3                      +   6

8   Find the totals.

   a   89 + 10 = ☐           b   26 + 20 = ☐

   c      68                  d      77
       + 20                      + 10

81

5 Working with numbers to 100

**Worked example 2**

3 + 7 = 10

Use this number sentence to help you write two number sentences to show complements of 20 and one number sentence to show complements of 100 using tens numbers.

13 + 7 = 20
3 + 17 = 20

*As 20 is 10 more than 10, we can just add 10 to one of the numbers and the total.*

30 + 70 = 100

*Change the ones to tens to make complements of 100.*

9   Use this number sentence to help you write two number sentences to show complements of 20 and one number sentence to show complements of 100 using tens numbers.

8 + 2 = 10.

_____   _____   _____

10  Use the number bonds for 6 to help you write four number sentences to show the complements of 60 using tens numbers.

5.1  Addition

11 Find the totals.

a   3 + 6 + 7 = ☐

b   0 + 7 + 10 = ☐

c   1 + 5 + 8 = ☐

d   2 + 9 + 5 = ☐

## Challenge

12 Find the totals.

a   58
  + 20
  ―――

b   62
  +  7
  ―――

c   46
  + 20
  ―――

d   83
  +  6
  ―――

e   55
  + 30
  ―――

f   71
  +  8
  ―――

13 Sofia writes 4 + 6 = 10 and 40 + 60 = 100.

Which number sentence showing complements of 20 could she use to help her?

_____

## 5 Working with numbers to 100

**14** Write the 5 number sentences which use tens numbers to show complements of 90.

**15** Find the totals. Look for complements of 10, or near complements, to help you.

7 + 3 + 8 = ☐        6 + 8 + 5 + 2 = ☐

2 + 3 + 4 + 5 = ☐        3 + 4 + 7 + 8 = ☐

5 + 6 + 7 + 8 = ☐        1 + 4 + 5 + 8 + 9 = ☐

Did you add the numbers in the same order as they are written or did you do something else?

Discuss different ways to find the totals with other learners.

5.1 Addition

16 Write the numbers 1, 2, 3, 4, 5, 6, 7, 8 and 9 in this square.

Every row, column and from corner to corner in the square must add to 15.

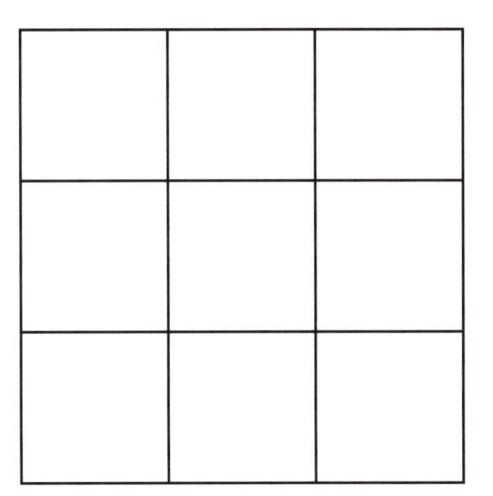

**Tip**

Think about how to make a total of 15 in every row and column, and from corner to corner. Remember 10 + 5 = 15.

Challenge your carer to complete this puzzle. Did they find the same solution as you?

5 Working with numbers to 100

## > 5.2 Subtraction

Exercise 5.2

> column subtraction    operation

**Focus**

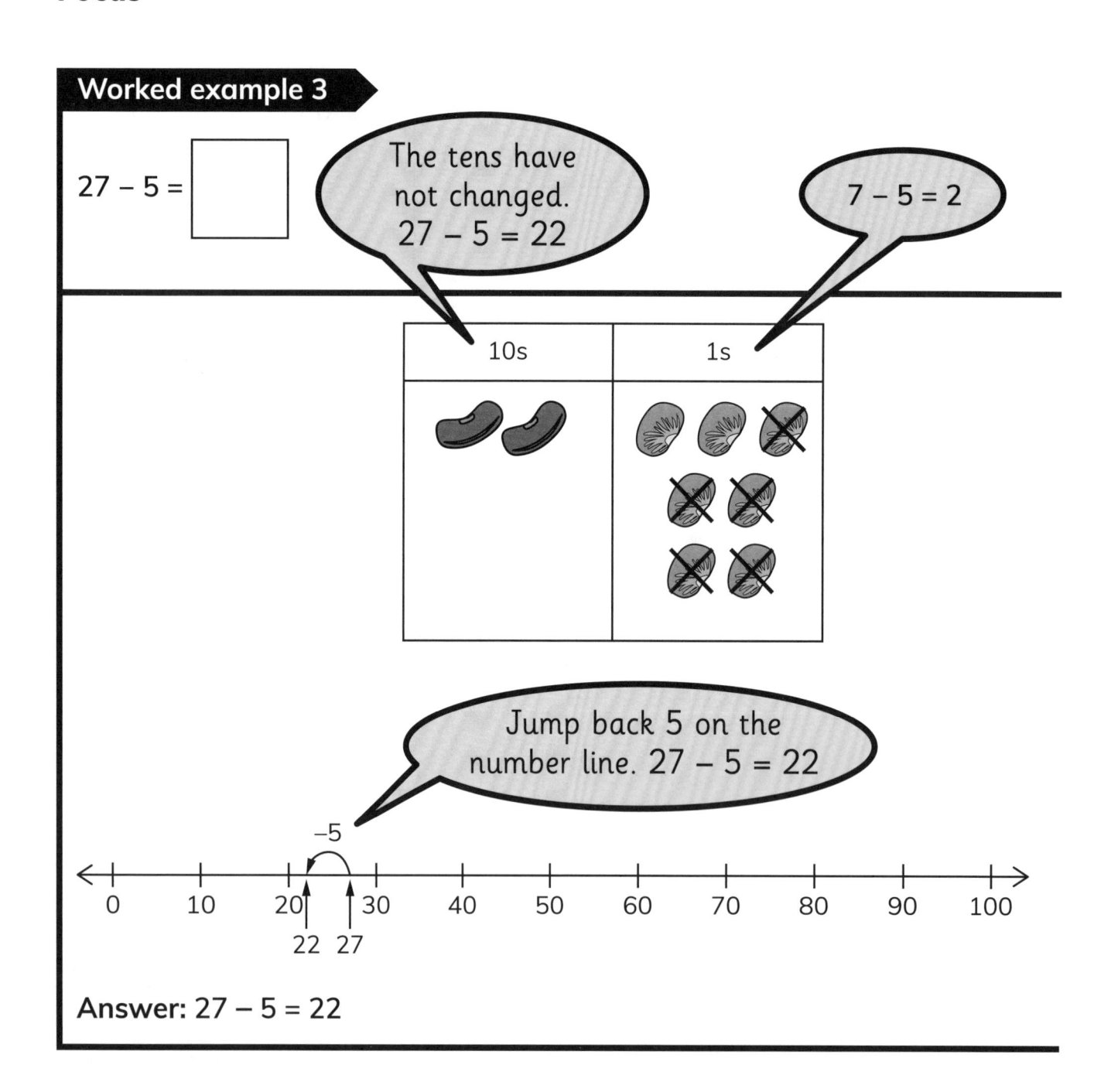

**Worked example 3**

27 − 5 = ☐

The tens have not changed.
27 − 5 = 22

7 − 5 = 2

| 10s | 1s |
|---|---|

Jump back 5 on the number line. 27 − 5 = 22

−5

0  10  20  30  40  50  60  70  80  90  100
     22 27

Answer: 27 − 5 = 22

86 >

5.2 Subtraction

1   Find the missing numbers. You can use the number line to help you.

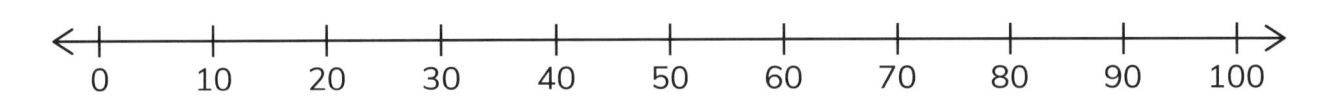

<--+----+----+----+----+----+----+----+----+----+----+-->
   0   10   20   30   40   50   60   70   80   90  100

a   39 − 8 = ☐      b   48 − 5 = ☐

c   77 − 5 = ☐      d   59 − 7 = ☐

2   Find the missing numbers. You can use the number line to help you.

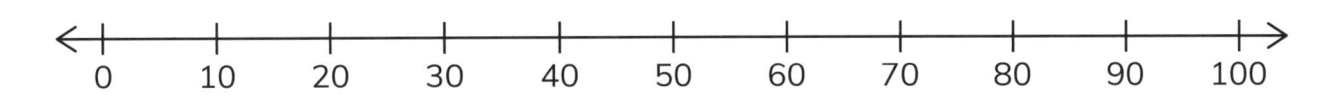

<--+----+----+----+----+----+----+----+----+----+----+-->
   0   10   20   30   40   50   60   70   80   90  100

a   24 − 10 = ☐     b   41 − 10 = ☐

c   52 − 20 = ☐     d   38 − 20 = ☐

3   Choose the correct operation (add or subtract) to solve each word problem. Write and solve your number sentence.

a   A farmer has 6 ducks and 22 ducklings.

    How many ducks and ducklings does she have altogether?

    _____

## 5 Working with numbers to 100

**b** There are 37 elephants in a herd. 5 of them are calves.
How many adult elephants are there?

_____

**4** Which calculation does not have the same answer as the others?
Draw a ring around that calculation.

27 − 3          14 + 10          34 − 10          29 − 4

Check your solution with another person. Do you both agree?

## 5.2 Subtraction

**Practice**

5   Find the missing numbers.

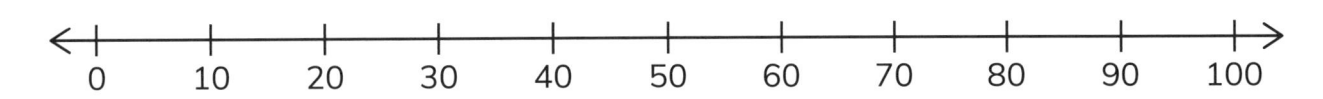

&larr;|—|—|—|—|—|—|—|—|—|—|&rarr;
0  10  20  30  40  50  60  70  80  90  100

a   57 − 4 = ☐         b   88 − 3 = ☐         c   69 − 5 = ☐

d     48              e     89              f     77
    −  5                  −  8                  −  7
    ‾‾‾                   ‾‾‾                   ‾‾‾

6   Find the missing numbers.

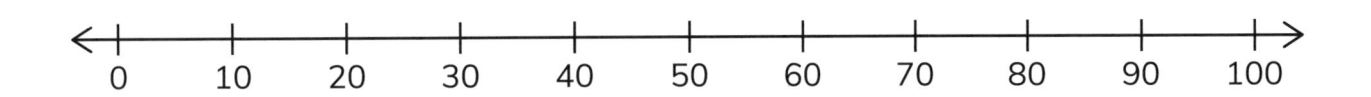

&larr;|—|—|—|—|—|—|—|—|—|—|&rarr;
0  10  20  30  40  50  60  70  80  90  100

a   57 − 10 = ☐        b   94 − 20 = ☐        c   66 − 30 = ☐

d     78              e     89              f     45
    − 10                  − 30                  − 20
    ‾‾‾                   ‾‾‾                   ‾‾‾

5 Working with numbers to 100

7 Choose the correct operation (add or subtract) to solve each word problem.

Write and solve your number sentence.

a There are 42 zebras in a herd. 20 of them are foals.

How many adult zebras are there?

_____

b There are 35 small balls and 30 large balls in the cupboard.

How many balls are there altogether?

_____

## 5.2 Subtraction

8  Tick any correct calculations. Correct any mistakes.

    45 − 20          52 + 40          32 + 5          99 − 8

$$\begin{array}{r} 45 \\ -\phantom{0}2 \\ \hline 43 \end{array} \qquad \begin{array}{r} 52 \\ -40 \\ \hline 12 \end{array} \qquad \begin{array}{r} 32 \\ +\phantom{0}5 \\ \hline 37 \end{array} \qquad \begin{array}{r} 99 \\ -80 \\ \hline 19 \end{array}$$

9  Sofia is thinking of a number.

When she adds 7 to her number, she gets 59.

What is Sofia's number?

**Tip**

Mark 59 on a number line then think about what Sofia does to get to 59.

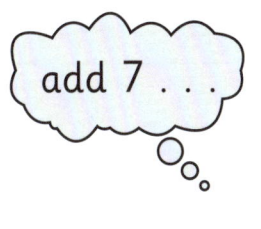

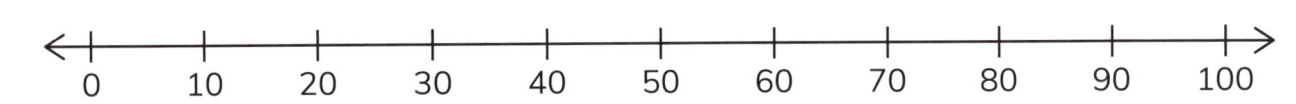

add 7 . . .

Talk to another learner or your carer about how you found Sofia's number.

## 5 Working with numbers to 100

## Challenge

10 Choose the correct operation (add or subtract) to solve each word problem. Write and solve your number sentence.

a   There are 68 strawberries growing in the garden.

Arun eats 5 strawberries.

How many strawberries are left?

_____  ☐

b   Zara collects 32 shells and 30 stones.

How many shells and stones does she collect altogether?

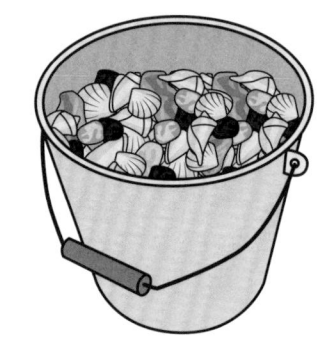

_____  ☐

5.2 Subtraction

11 Write the missing digits.

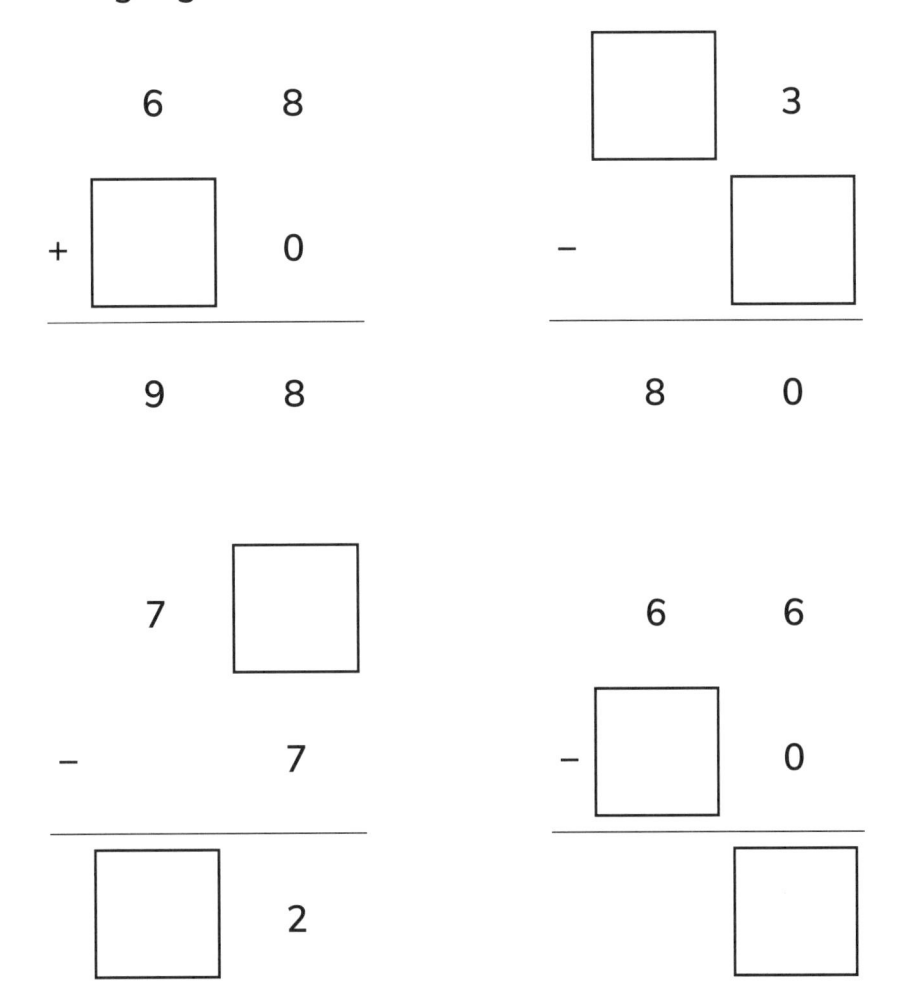

```
   6  8              ☐  3
+ ☐  0           -      ☐
  ─────            ─────
   9  8              8  0
```

```
   7  ☐              6  6
-     7           -  ☐  0
  ─────            ─────
   ☐  2              ☐
```

Talk to another learner or your carer about how you found the digits.

12 I am thinking of a number.

When I add 6 and subtract 30, I get 17.

What is my number?

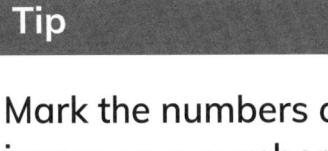

**Tip**

Mark the numbers and jumps on a number line to help you.

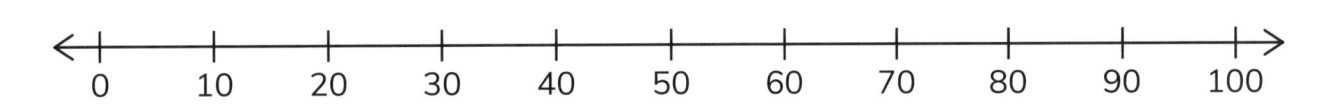

←|——|——|——|——|——|——|——|——|——|——|→
0  10  20  30  40  50  60  70  80  90  100

Talk to another learner or your carer about how you found my number.

93

5 Working with numbers to 100

## > 5.3 Multiplication

Exercise 5.3

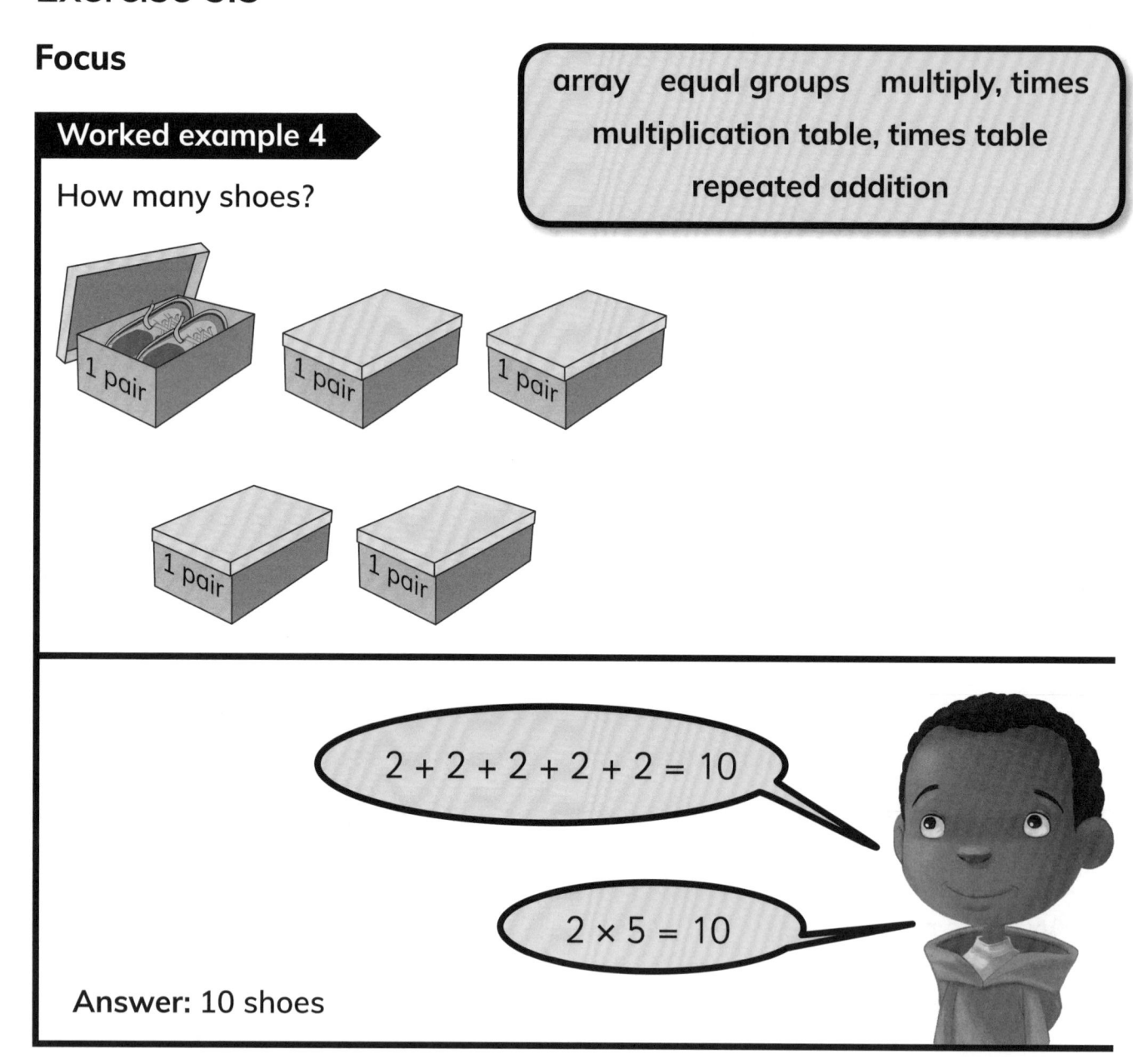

**Focus**

> array   equal groups   multiply, times
> multiplication table, times table
> repeated addition

**Worked example 4**

How many shoes?

[5 shoe boxes, each labelled "1 pair"]

$2 + 2 + 2 + 2 + 2 = 10$

$2 \times 5 = 10$

Answer: 10 shoes

94 >

5.3 Multiplication

1. How many legs? Write the number sentence you used to find the total.

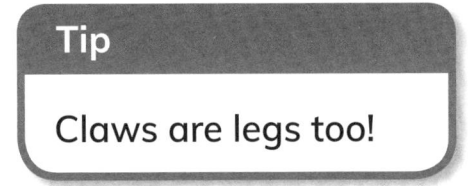

   **Tip**
   Claws are legs too!

   _____

2. How many toes on 4 feet? Write the number sentence you used to find the total.

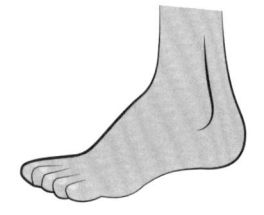

   _____

3. Write the repeated addition and multiplication number sentences for this number line.

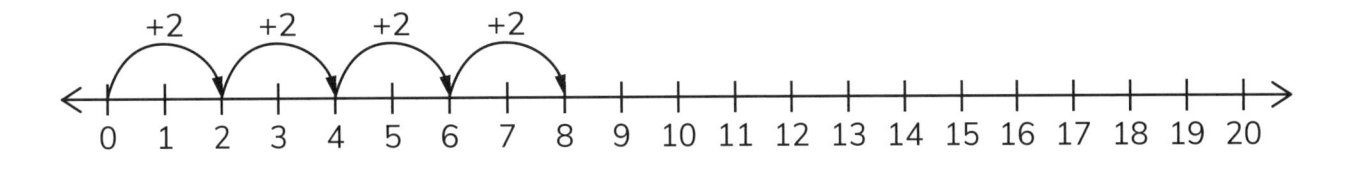

   _____

## 5 Working with numbers to 100

4  Write a multiplication sentence for each array.

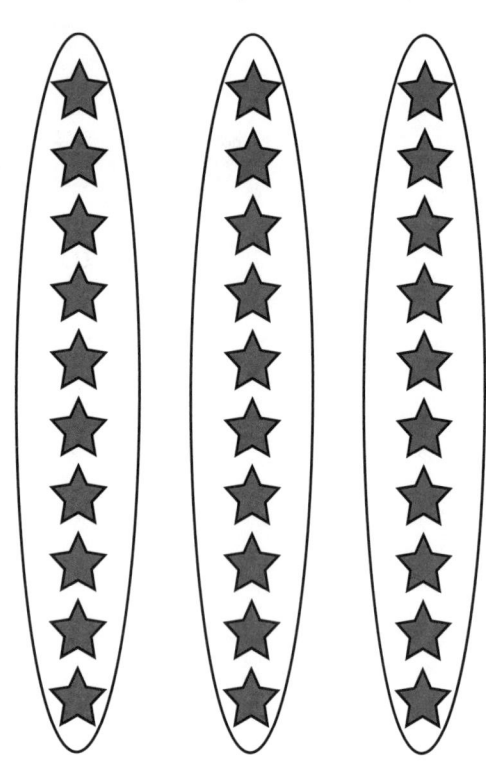

_____

_____

5  Draw an array to show that 5 × 4 = 20.

6   Write the multiplication table for 2. Go up to 2 × 10 = 20.

| □ × □ = □ | □ × □ = □ |
| □ × □ = □ | □ × □ = □ |
| □ × □ = □ | □ × □ = □ |
| □ × □ = □ | □ × □ = □ |
| □ × □ = □ | □ × □ = □ |

## Practice

7   Write the repeated addition and multiplication number sentences for this number line.

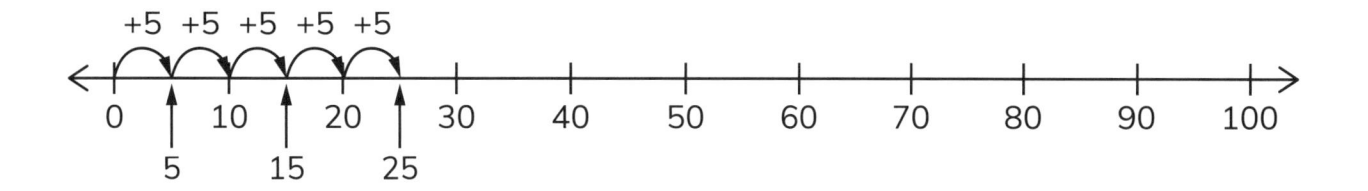

+5 +5 +5 +5 +5

0, 5, 10, 15, 20, 25, 30, 40, 50, 60, 70, 80, 90, 100

_____

_____

## 5 Working with numbers to 100

**8** Write the missing number sentences.

| Repeated addition | Multiplication |
|---|---|
|  | 10 × 1 = 10 |
| 10 + 10 + 10 = 30 |  |
|  | 5 × 8 = 40 |
| 5 + 5 + 5 + 5 + 5 + 5 = 30 |  |
|  | 2 × 6 = 12 |
| 2 + 2 = 4 |  |

**9** Draw an array for each multiplication.

2 × 9 = 18          5 × 6 = 30

98

10 Write the missing sentences.

| Double | Addition | Multiplication |
|---|---|---|
|  | 10 + 10 = 20 |  |
| double 1 is 2 |  |  |
|  |  | 2 × 2 = 4 |

11 Use the counting stick to help you find the correct answers.

What is the 3rd number you say when counting in twos from 0?

What is the 1st number you say when counting in fives from 0?

What is the 4th number you say when counting in tens from 0?

## 5 Working with numbers to 100

## Challenge

12  Complete this multiplication grid.

| × | 1 | 2 | 5 | 10 |
|---|---|---|---|---|
| 1 |   |   |   |   |
| 2 |   | 4 |   |   |
| 5 |   |   | 25 |   |
| 10 |   |   |   |   |

13  Use the counting stick to help you find the correct answers.

What is the 9th number you say when counting in fives from 0?

What is the 6th number you say when counting in tens from 0?

What is the 9th number you say when counting in twos from 0?

## 5.3 Multiplication

14 Complete the multiplication pyramids.

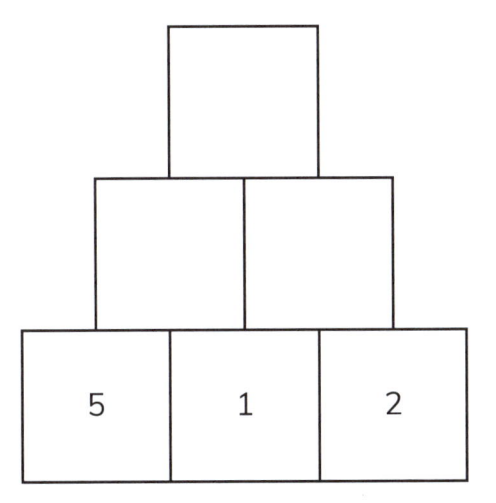

**Tip**

Multiply numbers next to each other to find the number above.

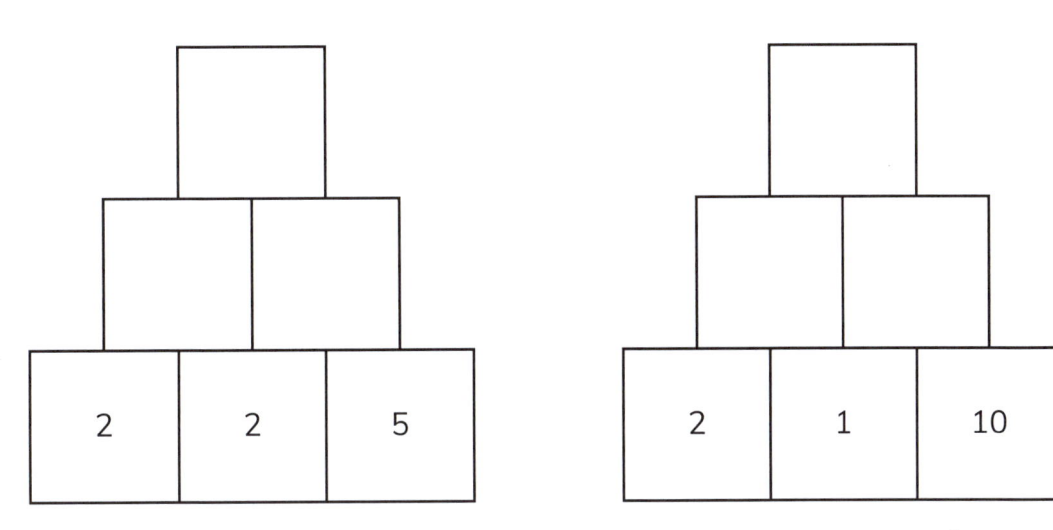

Pyramid 1 (bottom row): 5, 1, 2

Pyramid 2 (bottom row): 2, 2, 5

Pyramid 3 (bottom row): 2, 1, 10

Discuss with your partner or carer how you completed each pyramid.

5 Working with numbers to 100

## > 5.4 Division

Exercise 5.4

**Focus**

> division, divide   division as grouping
> division as sharing   repeated subtraction

**Worked example 5**

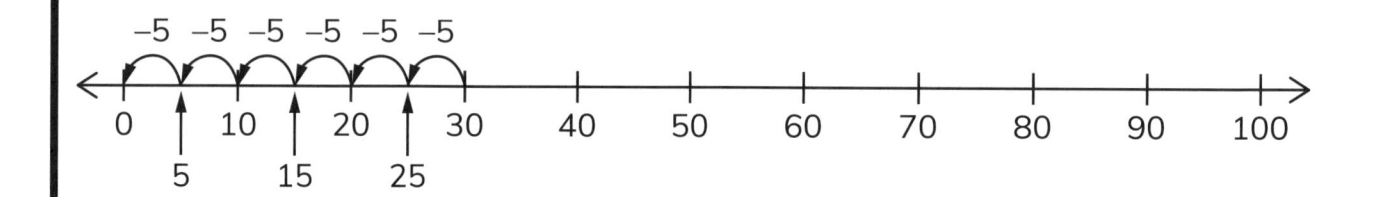

$30 \div 5 = \square$

−5 −5 −5 −5 −5 −5

0, 5, 10, 15, 20, 25, 30, 40, 50, 60, 70, 80, 90, 100

Start at 30 and keep taking away groups of 5 until you reach 0.

There are 6 groups of 5.
$30 \div 5 = 6$

Answer: $30 \div 5 = 6$

5.4 Division

1. Use repeated subtraction on the number line to help you solve each division.

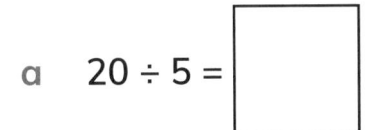

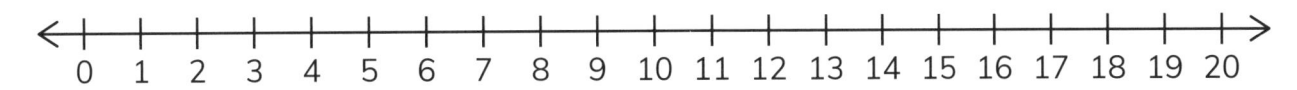

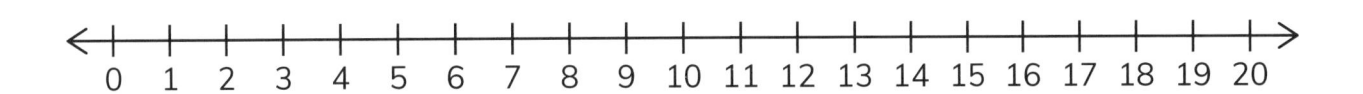

   a  $20 \div 5 = \boxed{\phantom{0}}$

   ←—+—+—+—+—+—+—+—+—+—+—+—+—+—+—+—+—+—+—+—+—→
   0  1  2  3  4  5  6  7  8  9  10 11 12 13 14 15 16 17 18 19 20

   b  $8 \div 2 = \boxed{\phantom{0}}$

   ←—+—+—+—+—+—+—+—+—+—+—+—+—+—+—+—+—+—+—+—+—→
   0  1  2  3  4  5  6  7  8  9  10 11 12 13 14 15 16 17 18 19 20

**Worked example 6**

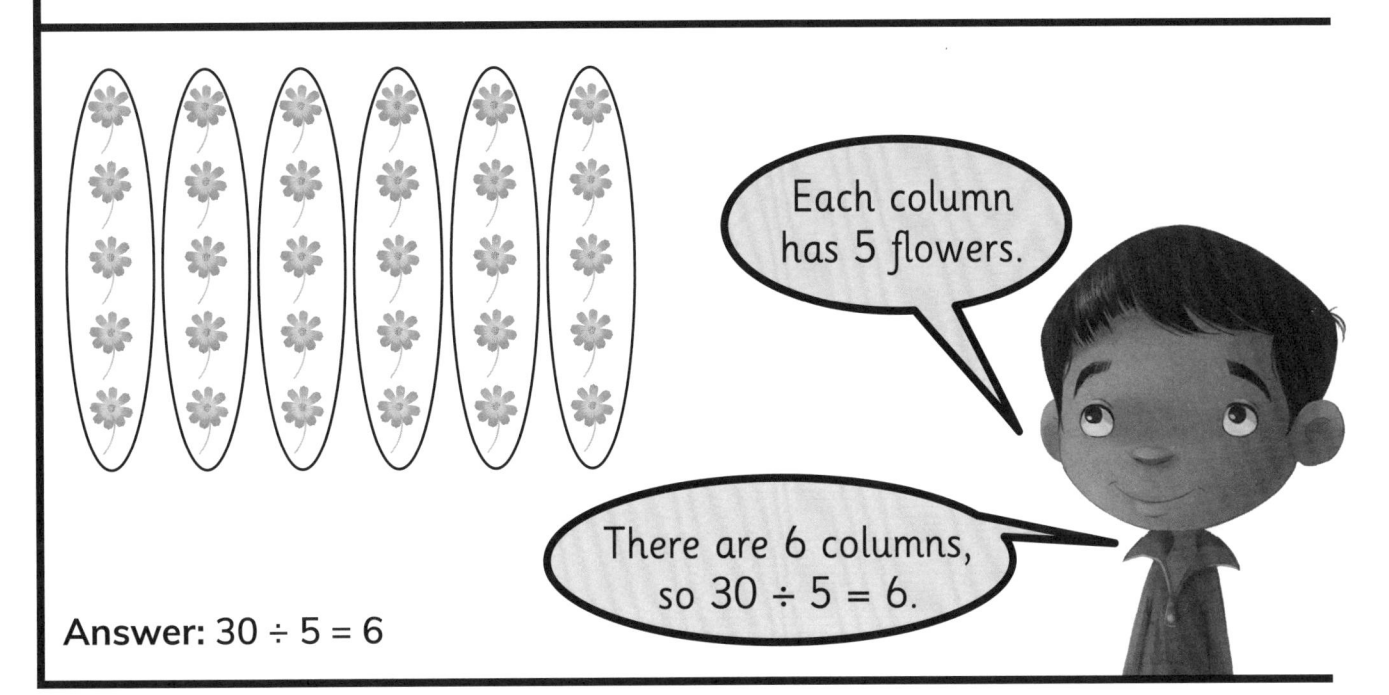

$30 \div 5 = \boxed{\phantom{0}}$

Each column has 5 flowers.

There are 6 columns, so $30 \div 5 = 6$.

Answer: $30 \div 5 = 6$

5 Working with numbers to 100

2 Use the array to help you solve each division.

a  20 ÷ 10 =

b  20 ÷ 2 =

**Tip**

Draw a ring around each group to help you.

3 Write a division number sentence for this array.

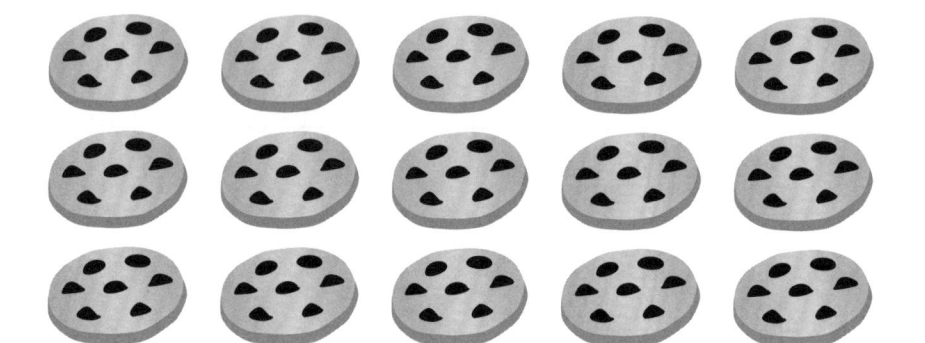

4 Share 20 marbles between 5 children.

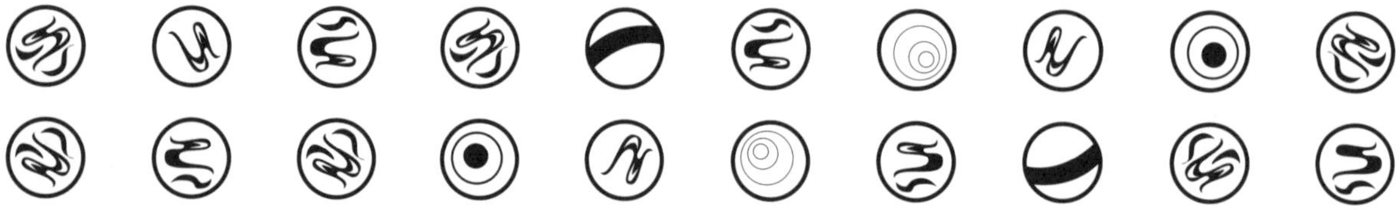

20 ÷ 5 =

104

5.4 Division

**Practice**

5   Use repeated subtraction on the number line to help you solve each division.

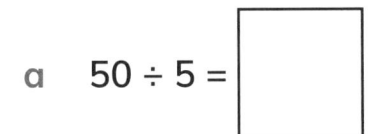

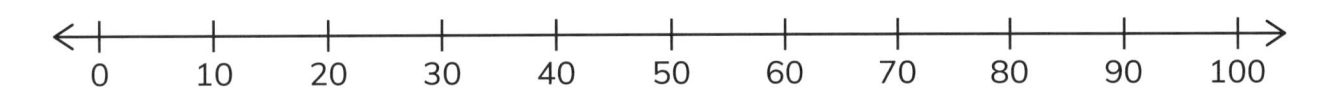

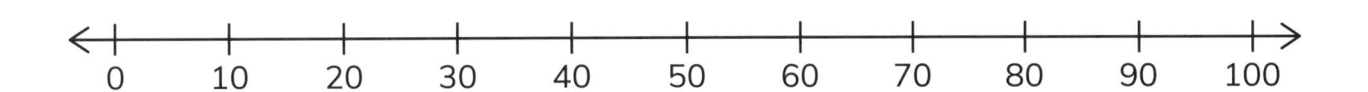

a   50 ÷ 5 = ☐

```
←—+—+—+—+—+—+—+—+—+—+—+→
  0  10 20 30 40 50 60 70 80 90 100
```

b   90 ÷ 10 = ☐

```
←—+—+—+—+—+—+—+—+—+—+—+→
  0  10 20 30 40 50 60 70 80 90 100
```

6   Draw a ring around the correct number sentence for this array.

**Tip**

How many cars are in the ringed group?

45 ÷ 9 = 9          45 ÷ 5 = 9          45 ÷ 5 = 5

105

5 Working with numbers to 100

7 Choose a method to use and find the answers.

a   12 ÷ 2 = ☐     b   40 ÷ 5 = ☐     c   70 ÷ 10 = ☐

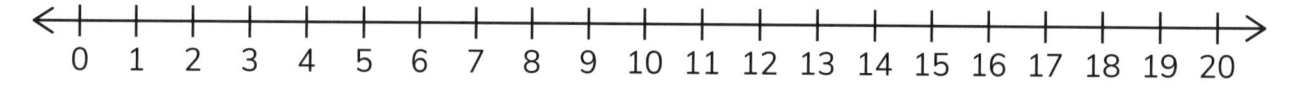

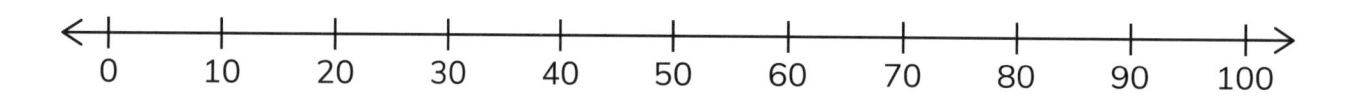

8 Write and solve the number sentences.
Do you need to multiply or divide?

a   Marcus rolls a dice 3 times.

He gets a 2 each time.

What is his total score?

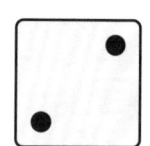

5.4 Division

b  18 children want to play football.

They choose 2 teams.

How many children in each team?

☐

## Challenge

9  Draw a ring around the two correct number sentences for this array.

30 ÷ 6 = 6      30 ÷ 5 = 6      30 ÷ 5 = 5      30 ÷ 6 = 5

## 5 Working with numbers to 100

10 Write and solve the number sentences.

Do you need to multiply or divide?

a  Egg cartons hold 10 eggs.

There are 100 eggs in a basket.

How many cartons do I need?

☐

b  How many wheels on 9 bicycles?

☐

11 Write a problem for this division number sentence.

60 ÷ 10 = 6

# 6 Money

## > 6.1 Money

> currency   dollar, cent   euro, euro cent
> pound sterling, pence   price
> unit of money   value   worth   yen

### Exercise 6.1

**Focus**

1 Count in tens. What is the total value of these coins?

2 Marcus uses a Carroll diagram to sort US$ banknotes.
  Which banknotes are missing from each section?

| Even value | Not even value |
|---|---|

6 Money

**Worked example 1**

Arun spends 30c on some candy. Which coins could he pay with?

**Answer:**

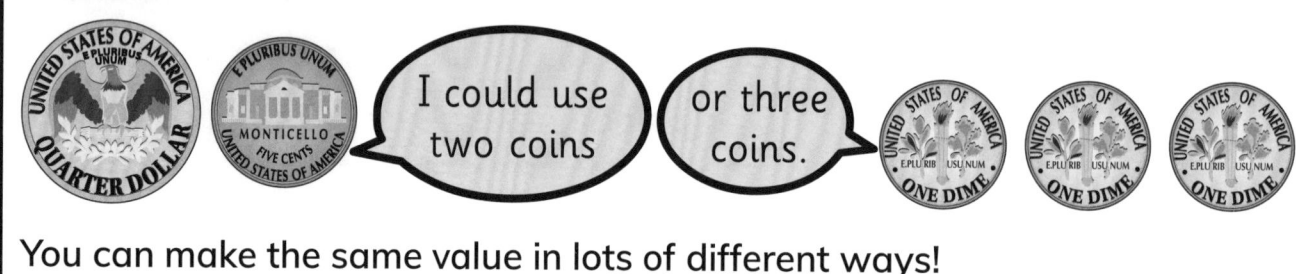

"I could use two coins" "or three coins."

You can make the same value in lots of different ways!

3   Sofia spends 25c on some candy.

   Show one way she could pay using coins.

   Find another way to pay.

**Worked example 2**

Sofia spends US$15 on a T-shirt. Which banknotes could Sofia pay with?

**Answer:**

1 US$10 and 1 US$5 banknotes

3 US$5 banknotes

You can make the same value in lots of different ways!

110

6.1 Money

4   Zara spends US$30 on some books.

Show one way she could pay using banknotes.

Find another way to pay.

> **Worked example 3**
>
> Arun spends US$6 and 70c in the supermarket.
>
> Which banknotes and coins could he pay with?
>
> Answer: 
>
> US$5, US$1, a half dollar and 2 dimes
>
> 3 US$2 and 7 dimes
>
> You can make the same value in lots of different ways!

6 Money

5   Arun spends US$5 and 45c in the supermarket.

Show one way he could pay using banknotes and coins.

**Practice**

6   Count in fives. What is the total value of these coins?

7   Sofia sorts US currency. How should she label her circle?

6.1 Money

## Worked example 4

Zara's mum spends US$57 and 90c in the supermarket.

Which banknotes and coins could she pay with?

Answer:

US$50, US$5, US$2, 3 quarter dollars, a dime and a nickel

5 US$10, US$5, US$2, a half dollar, a quarter dollar and 3 nickels

You can make the same value in lots of different ways!

# 6 Money

8  Marcus' dad spends US$62 and 15c in the supermarket.

Which banknotes and coins could he pay with?

Find another way to pay.

## Challenge

9  Arun matches a US$1 banknote and 1c coin because they both have 'one' on them. Which other matches could Arun make with US currency?

10  Sofia has 5 silver coins.

Marcus has 3 silver coins.

They both have the same amount of money.

Which coins could they each have? Use US dollars and cents or your own currency.

Find another solution.

Discuss your answers with a partner or carer.
Have you found all the possible answers?

6.1 Money

11  Complete the table of currency symbols.

There are two empty rows in the table for you to complete if you know any more currencies.

| Country or region | Lower value unit | Higher value unit |
|---|---|---|
| Your country | | |
| USA | | |
| | | € |
| Japan | none | |
| | p | £ |
| | | |
| | | |

# 7 Time

## > 7.1 Units of time and the calendar

**Exercise 7.1**

> calendar   date   second
> units of time   weekend   year

**Focus**

1   Name 3 things that take about an hour.

_____

_____

_____

**Worked example 1**

Put these units of time in order from shortest to longest.

hour     month     minute     week

> A minute is a lot shorter than an hour.

> A month is about 4 weeks, so a month is longer than a week. A week is a lot longer than an hour.

Answer: The order must be:

minute     hour     week     month

7.1 Units of time and the calendar

2  Put these units of time in order from the shortest to the longest.

year        month        minute        second        hour

_____       _____        _____         _____         _____

3  How many days in a week? _____

   How many months in a year? _____

4  Write the ordinal number for each of the days.

June

| M | T | W | T | F | S | S |
|---|---|---|---|---|---|---|
|   |   | 1 | 2 | 3 | 4 | 5 |
| 6 | 7 | 8 | 9 | 10 | 11 | 12 |
| 13 | 14 | 15 | 16 | 17 | 18 | 19 |
| 20 | 21 | 22 | 23 | 24 | 25 | 26 |
| 27 | 28 | 29 | 30 |   |   |   |

The first Thursday in June is the _____ .

The last Wednesday in June is the _____ .

The third Tuesday in June is the _____ .

The first Sunday in June is the _____ .

117

## 7 Time

**Worked example 2**

Look at the calendar in question 5. Write this date in words: 22/11/21.

> The 11th month is November. 22 is in the column with M for Monday at the top. The 22nd November is a Monday.

> 22/11/21 is Monday 22nd November, 2021.

5   Write these dates in words.

**2021**

**November**

| M | T | W | T | F | S | S |
|---|---|---|---|---|---|---|
| 1 | 2 | 3 | 4 | 5 | 6 | 7 |
| 8 | 9 | 10 | 11 | 12 | 13 | 14 |
| 15 | 16 | 17 | 18 | 19 | 20 | 21 |
| 22 | 23 | 24 | 25 | 26 | 27 | 28 |
| 29 | 30 | | | | | |

**December**

| M | T | W | T | F | S | S |
|---|---|---|---|---|---|---|
| | | 1 | 2 | 3 | 4 | 5 |
| 6 | 7 | 8 | 9 | 10 | 11 | 12 |
| 13 | 14 | 15 | 16 | 17 | 18 | 19 |
| 20 | 21 | 22 | 23 | 24 | 25 | 26 |
| 27 | 28 | 29 | 30 | 31 | | |

a   12/11/21

b   05/12/21

c   30/11/21

**Tip**

Remember to write the day of the week for each date.

6 Write these dates in numbers only.

    a    Monday 13th July 2020 _____

    b    Saturday 11th September 2021 _____

    c    Wednesday 23rd February 2022 _____

7 Write today's date in numbers.

_____

Write yesterday's date and tomorrow's date in words.

_____

_____

## Practice

8 Name:
- something that takes about a minute
- something that takes about a second
- something that takes about an hour.

Write them in order, from shortest to longest.

_____

_____

_____

# 7 Time

9 Write the ordinal number for each of these days.

January

| M | T | W | T | F | S | S |
|---|---|---|---|---|---|---|
|   |   |   |   |   | 1 | 2 |
| 3 | 4 | 5 | 6 | 7 | 8 | 9 |
| 10 | 11 | 12 | 13 | 14 | 15 | 16 |
| 17 | 18 | 19 | 20 | 21 | 22 | 23 |
| 24 | 25 | 26 | 27 | 28 | 29 | 30 |
| 31 |   |   |   |   |   |   |

a The first Saturday in January is the _____ .

b The last Monday in January is the _____ .

c The third Friday in January is the _____ .

d The fifth Sunday in January is the _____ .

7.1 Units of time and the calendar

10 Write each of the ringed dates from 2022 in words and in numbers.

May

| M | T | W | T | F | S | S |
|---|---|---|---|---|---|---|
|   |   |   |   |   |   | 1 |
| 2 | 3 | 4 | 5 | 6 | 7 | 8 |
| 9 | 10 | 11 | 12 | 13 | 14 | 15 |
| 16 | 17 | 18 | 19 | 20 | 21 | 22 |
| 23 | 24 | 25 | 26 | 27 | 28 | 29 |
| 30 | 31 |   |   |   |   |   |

June

| M | T | W | T | F | S | S |
|---|---|---|---|---|---|---|
|   |   | 1 | 2 | 3 | 4 | 5 |
| 6 | 7 | 8 | 9 | 10 | 11 | 12 |
| 13 | 14 | 15 | 16 | 17 | 18 | 19 |
| 20 | 21 | 22 | 23 | 24 | 25 | 26 |
| 27 | 28 | 29 | 30 |   |   |   |

_____

_____

_____

_____

11 Write the missing months.

a  The month after June is _____ .

b  The month before October is _____ .

c  Two months before April is _____ .

d  Three months after August is _____ .

# 7 Time

## Challenge

**12** Put these units of time in order from **longest** to **shortest**.

second    weekend    minute    week    year    month    hour    day

_____

**13** In which month or months of 2022 will you find:

Thursday 8th? _____

Monday 30th? _____

Friday 12th? _____

7.1 Units of time and the calendar

Write the date in words for the day after 31/12/22.

_____

Write the date in words for the day before 01/01/22.

_____

Explain to a partner or carer how you found the dates.

14 Today is Friday 15th May.

Zara is going to a party in 2 weeks' time.

What is the date of the party in words?

_____

15 Marcus visits his grandfather on Saturday 24th July.

Marcus visits his grandfather again 3 weeks later.

Write the date of this visit in words.

_____

# 8 Numbers to 100 (2)

## > 8.1 Numbers in words, rounding and regrouping

> closest 10   hyphen   nearest 10
> regroup   round, rounding

### Exercise 8.1

**Focus**

1   Write each of the numbers represented below in words.

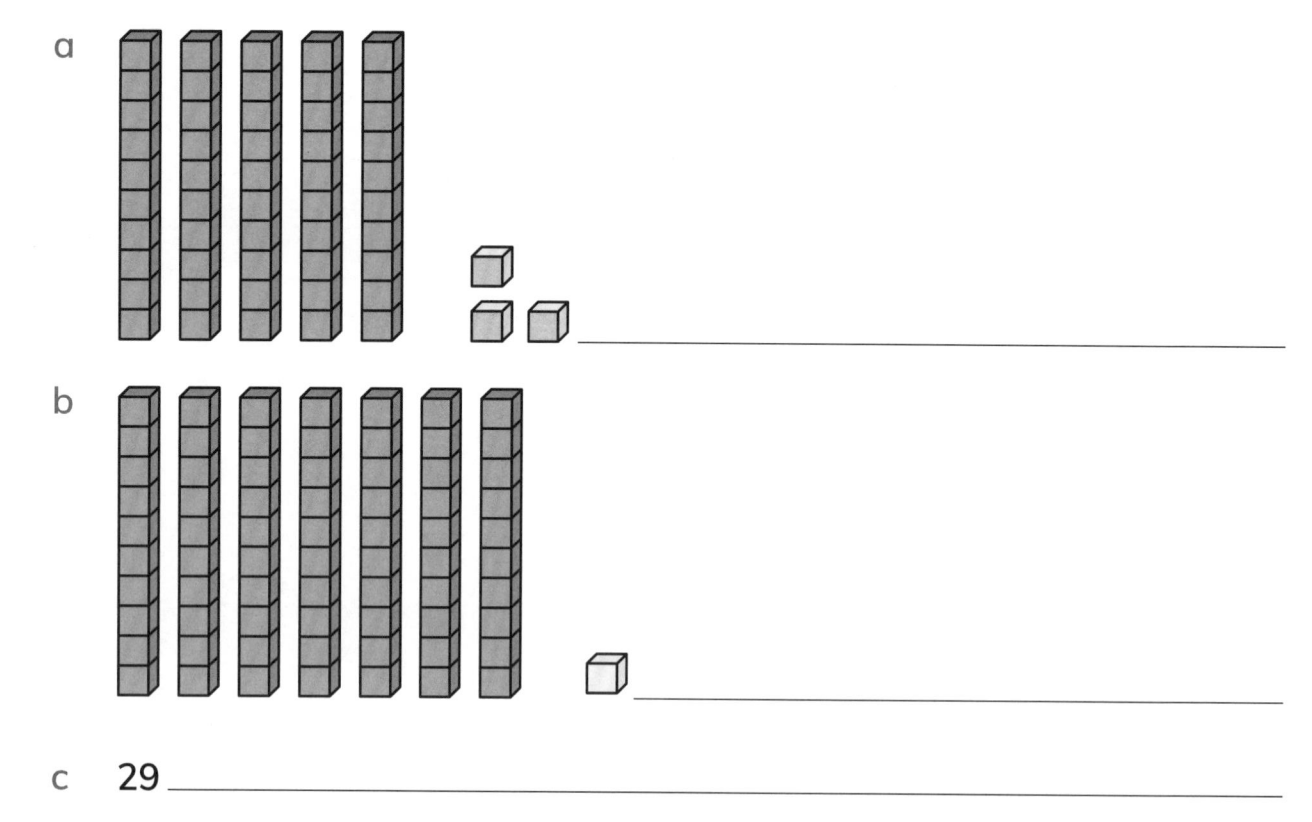

   a   

   b   

   c   29 _____

   d   47 _____

8.1 Numbers in words, rounding and regrouping

2  Read the number words and write the number.

   a  eighty-six _____              b  thirty-four _____

   c  forty-seven _____             d  sixty-two _____

3  Represent each number by drawing counters on the place value grid.

   a  forty-one                     b  thirty-six

   | 10s | 1s |
   |-----|----|
   |     |    |

   | 10s | 1s |
   |-----|----|
   |     |    |

4  Round each number to the nearest 10.

   a  51 ☐        b  68 ☐        c  45 ☐

   d  37 ☐        e  25 ☐        f  92 ☐

## 8 Numbers to 100 (2)

5. Find 4 different ways to regroup 24.

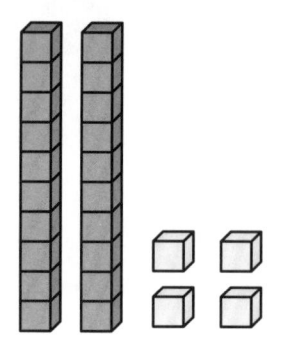

   Show another person your ways to group 24.
   Do they have any different ways?

## Practice

6. Use these number words to write some 2-digit numbers in words. How many different numbers can you write?

   five     fifty     four     ninety     sixty     one

7. A number rounds to 50 when rounded to the nearest 10. When 1 is added to the number, it now rounds to 60 when rounded to the nearest 10. What is the number?

8.1 Numbers in words, rounding and regrouping

8   Zara rounds 50 to 60 when rounding to the nearest 10.

    Zara remembers that 5 always rounds up.

    How can you help Zara to understand her mistake?

    _____

9   Find 4 different ways to regroup 35 into 3 numbers.

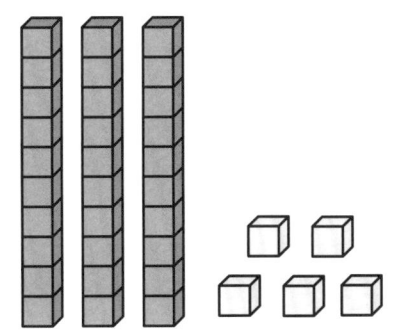

## Challenge

10  Write your answers in words.

    a   Forty-two add twenty equals          _____

    b   Seventy-six subtract five equals     _____

    c   Fifty-one add eight equals           _____

    d   Ninety-seven subtract fifty equals   _____

8 Numbers to 100 (2)

11 Write each calculation in words.

a   37
   + 20
   ___
    57   _____

   _____

b   99
   −  7
   ___
    92   _____

   _____

12 Round each length to the nearest 10 centimetres.

58 centimetres  _____ centimetres

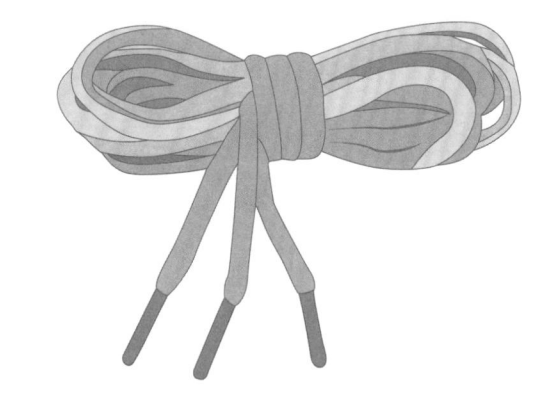

94 centimetres  _____ centimetres

128

13 Round each measurement to the nearest 10 metres.

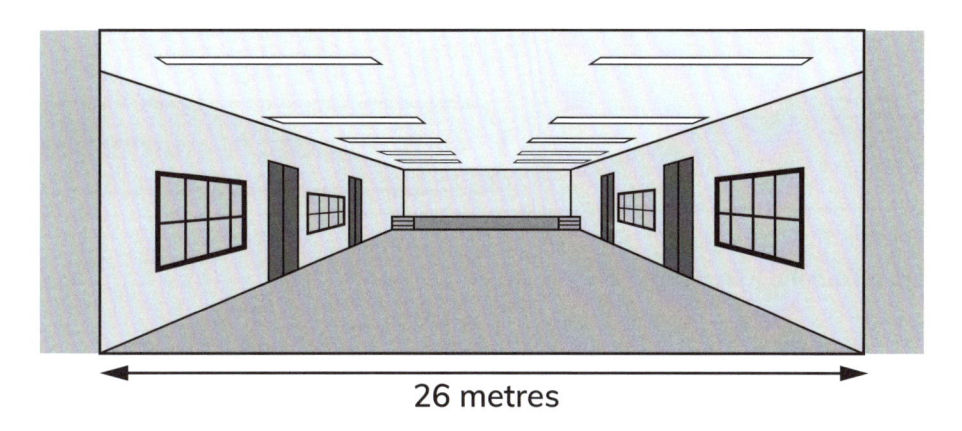

26 metres

_____ metres

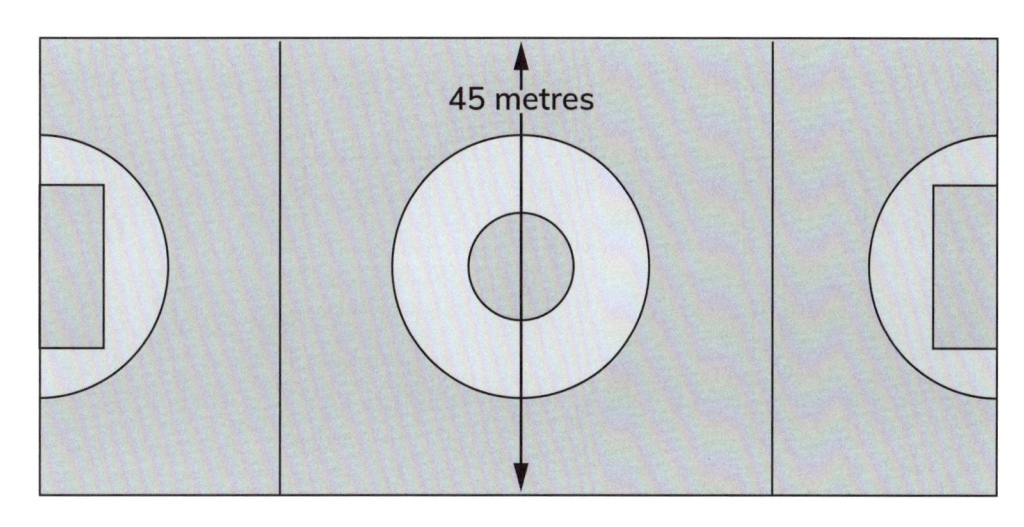

45 metres

_____ metres

14 When 49 is regrouped into 3 numbers, one of the numbers is 23. What could the other numbers be?

8 Numbers to 100 (2)

# > 8.2 Fractions of numbers

**Exercise 8.2**

denominator   numerator   visualise

**Focus**

1 Find the missing numbers.

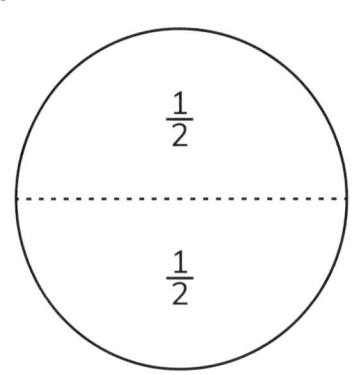

a  $\frac{1}{2}$ of 2 = ☐

b  $\frac{1}{2}$ of 4 = ☐

c  6 ÷ 2 = ☐

d  8 ÷ 2 = ☐

e  10 ÷ 2 = ☐

f  $\frac{1}{2}$ of 14 = ☐

2 Colour half of the shape.

Complete the number sentences.

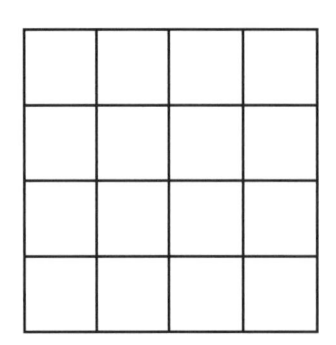

**Tip**

Count the squares!

a  ☐ ÷ 2 = ☐

b  $\frac{1}{2}$ of ☐ = ☐

8.2 Fractions of numbers

3 Find the missing numbers.

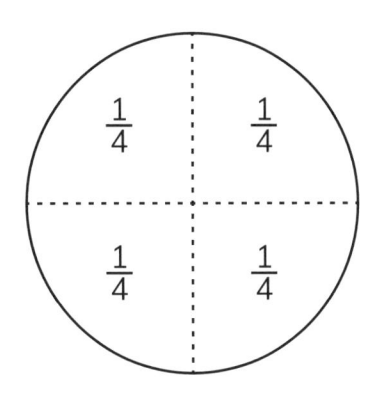

(circle divided into four quarters, each labelled $\frac{1}{4}$)

a  $\frac{1}{4}$ of 4 = ☐

b  8 ÷ 4 = ☐

c  12 ÷ 4 = ☐

d  20 ÷ 4 = ☐

e  $\frac{1}{4}$ of 20 = ☐

f  $\frac{1}{4}$ of 8 = ☐

4 Colour a quarter of the shape.

Complete the number sentences.

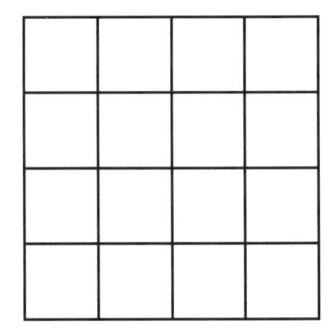

a  ☐ ÷ 4 = ☐

b  $\frac{1}{4}$ of ☐ = ☐

# 8 Numbers to 100 (2)

## Practice

5   Sofia and Zara share a pack of 16 beads equally.

   What fraction of the beads do they get each?

   _____

6   What is the number below the line in a fraction called?

   What does it represent?

   _____

7   You are given a quarter of a packet of 20 marbles.

   Draw your marbles.

   ┌─────────────────────────────────────────────┐
   │                                             │
   │                                             │
   │                                             │
   └─────────────────────────────────────────────┘

8   Half of a number is 1. What is the number? ☐

9   A quarter of a number is 5. What is the number? ☐

10   Dad cuts some apples into quarters for everyone to share.

   Sofia eats 2 quarters of green apple and a quarter of red apple.

   What fraction of an apple does she eat altogether?

11   Marcus eats 4 quarters of green apple.

   What fraction of an apple does he eat altogether?

## Challenge

12  Find the missing numbers.

$\frac{1}{2}$ of a number is 6. What is $\frac{1}{4}$ of that number?  _____

$\frac{1}{4}$ of a number is 4. What is $\frac{1}{2}$ of that number?  _____

13  Tick the calculations that have the same value as $\frac{1}{2}$ of 12.

$\frac{1}{4}$ of 12        $\frac{2}{4}$ of 12        12 ÷ 4 = 3        12 ÷ 2 = 6

14  Arun uses the round beads, Marcus uses the square beads and Zara uses the triangle beads.

What fraction of the beads does Marcus use?

What fraction of the beads does Zara use?

What fraction of the beads do Arun and Zara use altogether?

8 Numbers to 100 (2)

15 Mum makes sandwiches for the party.
All the whole sandwiches are the same size.
She cuts each sandwich into 4 equal pieces.

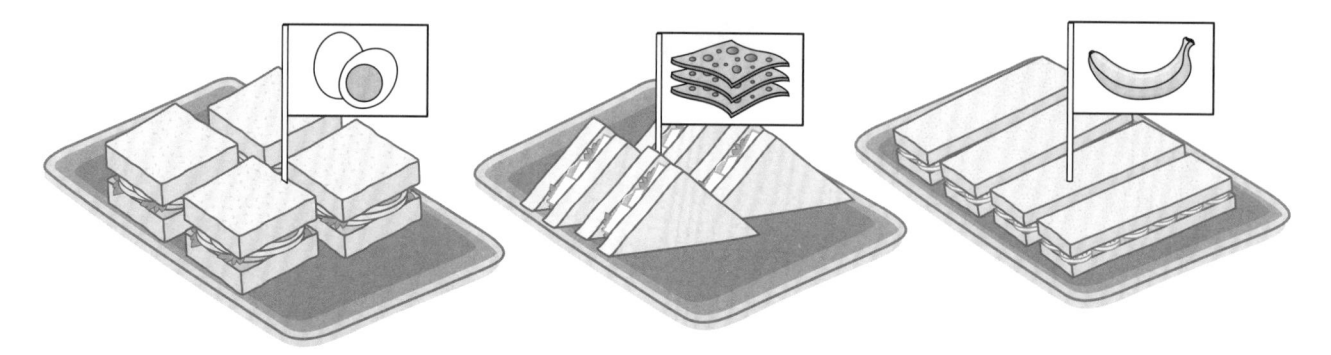

a Arun eats 1 banana sandwich strip and 1 cheese sandwich triangle. What fraction of a whole sandwich does he eat?

b Dad is really hungry. He eats 2 whole sandwiches. How many pieces does he eat?
Can he choose any pieces?

16 You have a US$1 banknote.
How can you give your friend a quarter of a dollar?

# 9 Statistics (2)

## > 9.1 Venn diagrams, lists and tables

Exercise 9.1

**Focus**

> Venn diagram

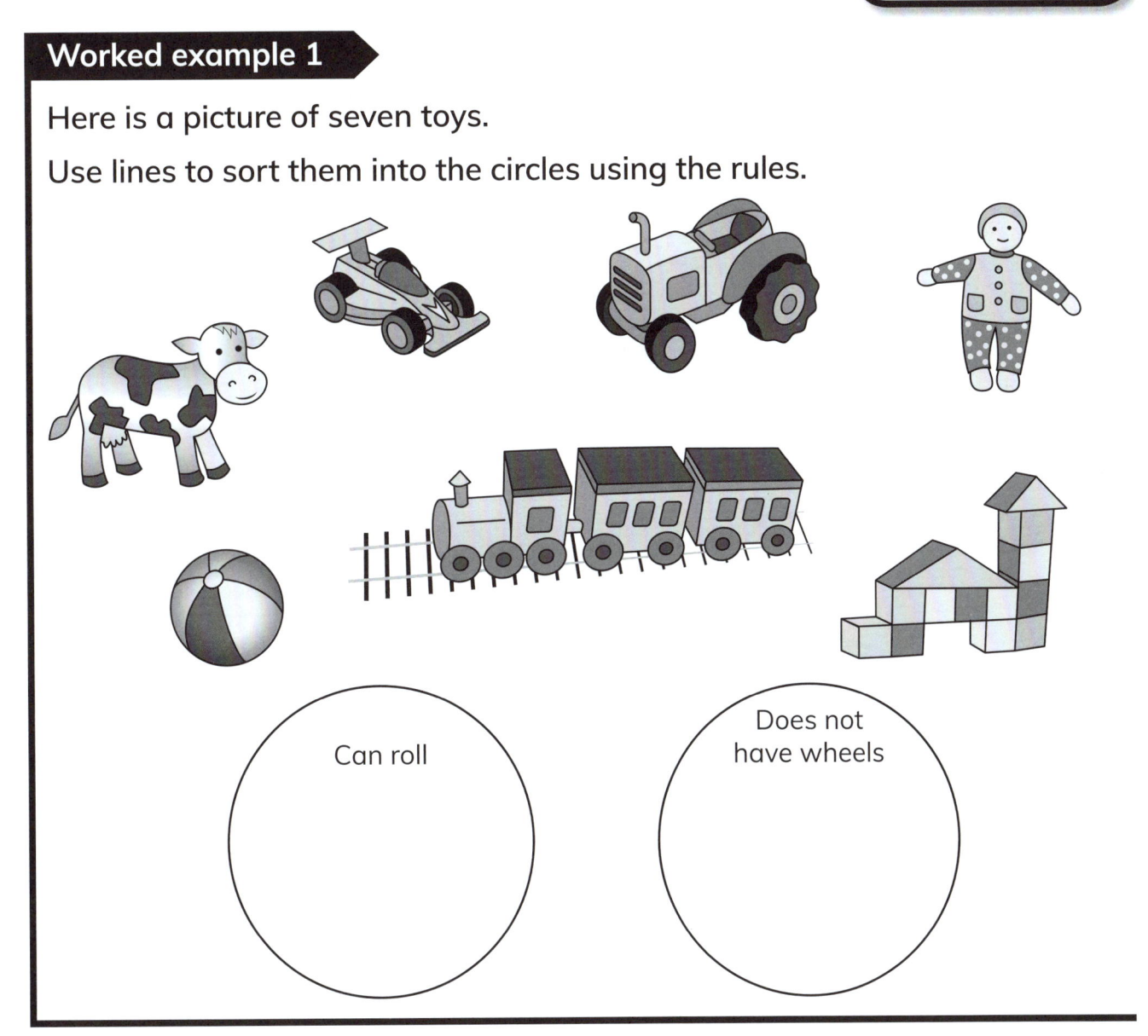

**Worked example 1**

Here is a picture of seven toys.

Use lines to sort them into the circles using the rules.

Can roll

Does not have wheels

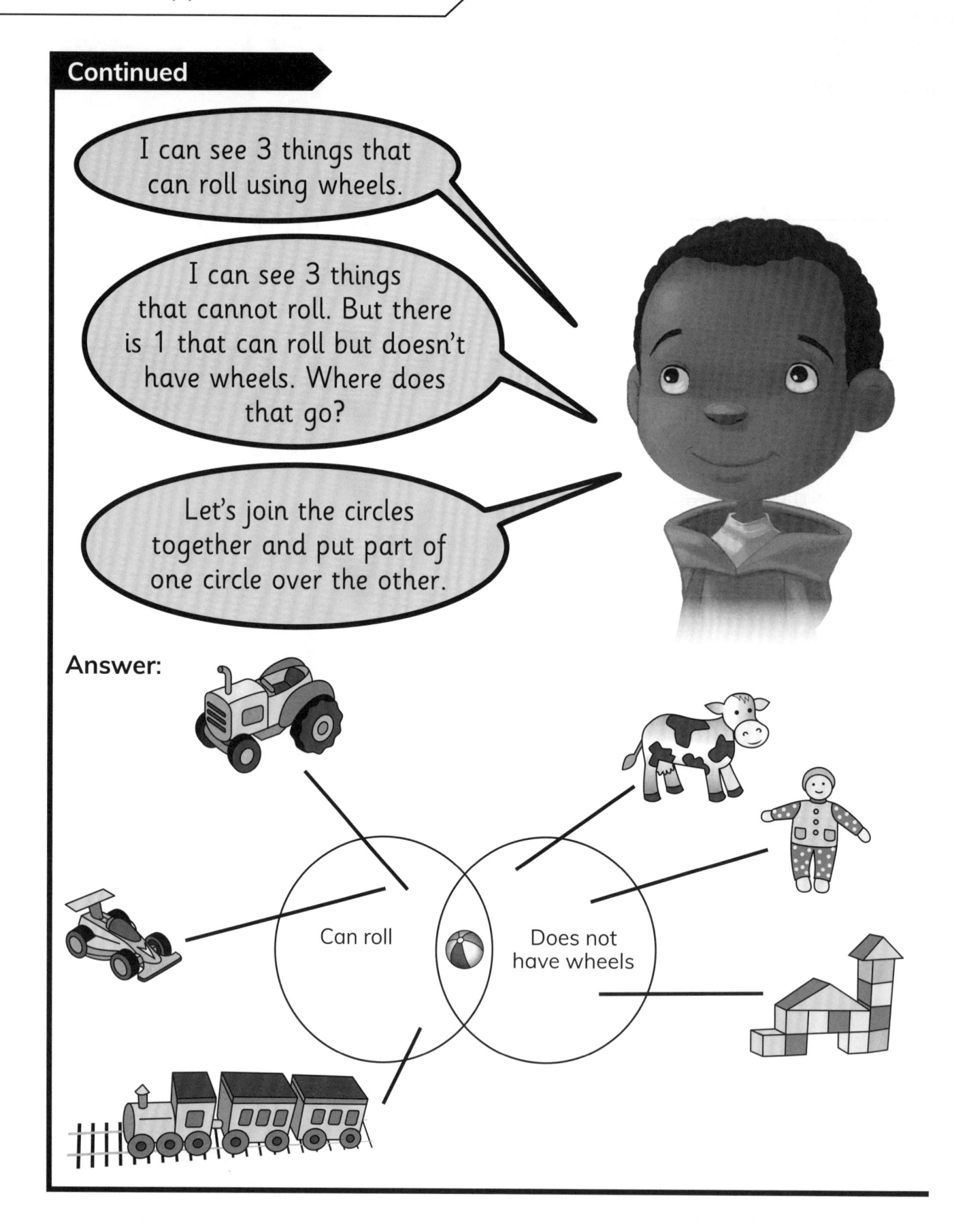

# 9 Statistics (2)

**Continued**

> I can see 3 things that can roll using wheels.

> I can see 3 things that cannot roll. But there is 1 that can roll but doesn't have wheels. Where does that go?

> Let's join the circles together and put part of one circle over the other.

Answer:

Can roll | Does not have wheels

9.1 Venn diagrams, lists and tables

1  Look at these numbers:

25, 9, 13, 62, 78, 21

Write them in the correct place in the Venn diagram.

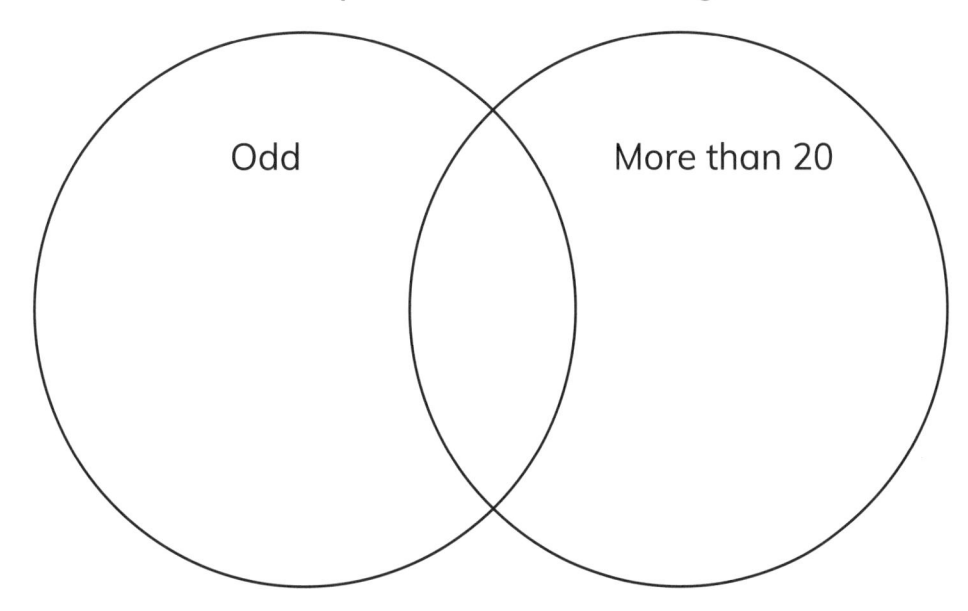

Odd          More than 20

2  Write the labels for the Venn diagram.

## 9 Statistics (2)

3  Make a list of 6 different foods that you buy in a shop.

Use the list to complete the table.

| Vegetables | Not vegetables |
|---|---|
|  |  |
|  |  |
|  |  |
|  |  |

How many vegetables are there? ☐

How many are not vegetables? ☐

How many are there altogether? ☐

9.1 Venn diagrams, lists and tables

## Practice

4   Use this table to complete the Venn diagram.

Draw the fruits and vegetables in the correct section of the Venn diagram.

| Red | Green | Red and green | Red | Green | Red and green |
|---|---|---|---|---|---|
| (apple) | (apple) | (apple) | (strawberry) | (lemon) | (mango) |
| Red | Red | Red | Green | Green | Green |
| (cherries) | (pepper) | (tomato) | (avocado) | (kiwi) | (broccoli) |

Red           Green

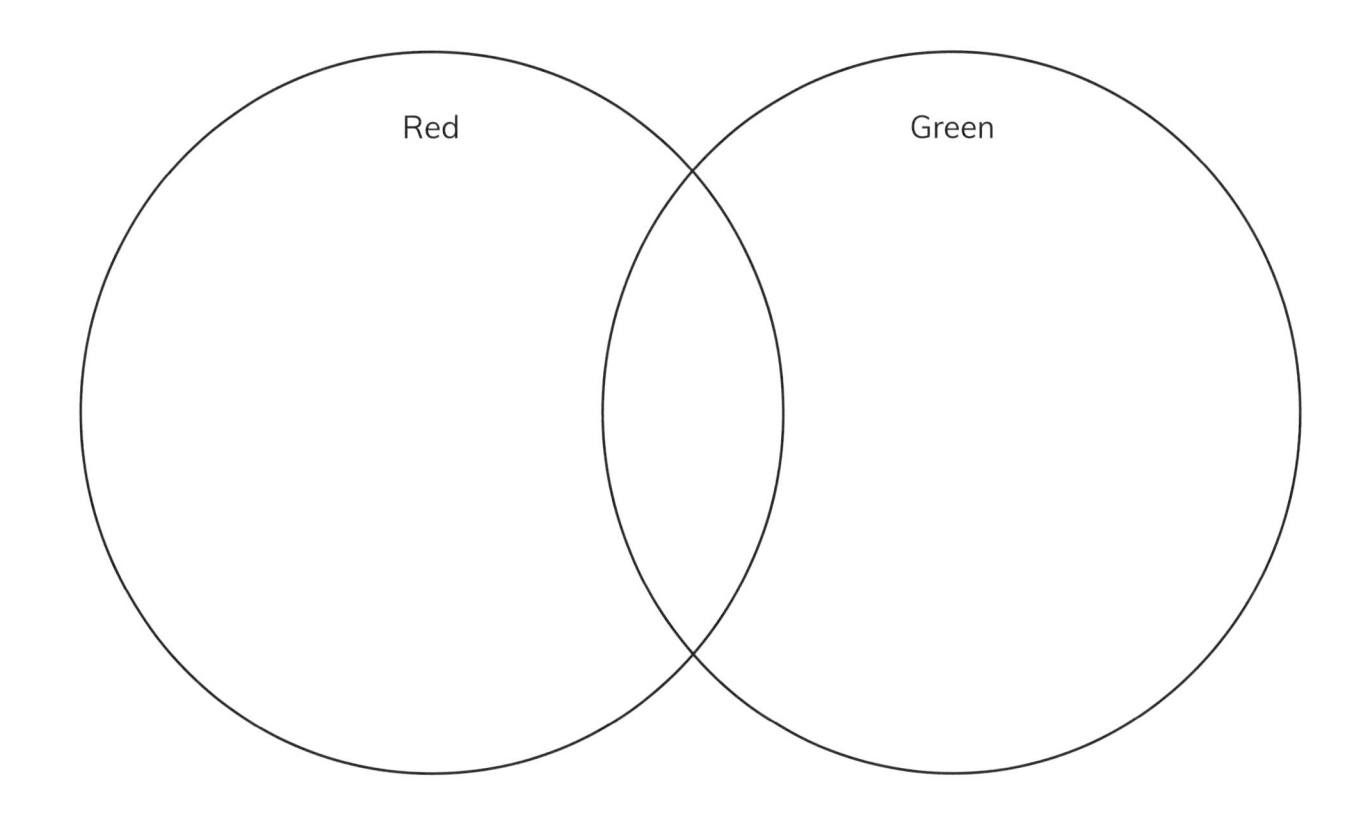

139

## 9 Statistics (2)

5   Zara asks boys what they like doing when they are not at school.

Answer the questions using the Venn diagram.

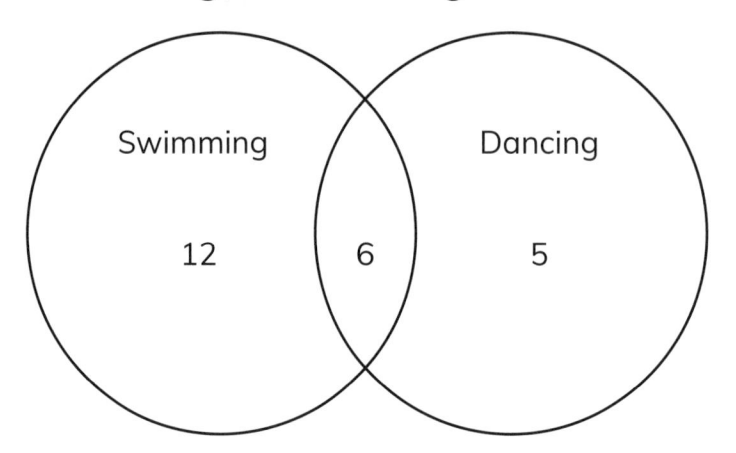

Swimming    Dancing

12    6    5

How many boys:

like both swimming and dancing? ☐

do not like dancing? ☐

do not like swimming? ☐

How many boys are there altogether? ☐

6   Arun needs to buy these foods for his dinner.

Would you use a list or a table to show this information?

Explain your choice.

_____

_____

## Challenge

7   The table shows data about the cats in the cat shelter.

Use the table to complete the Venn diagram. Write the cats' names.

|  | **Magic** | **Jack** | **Poppy** | **Tilly** | **Scrumpy** | **Monty** |
|---|---|---|---|---|---|---|
| **Hair colour** | grey | brown | grey | grey | grey | white |
| **Size** | large | large | small | small | large | large |

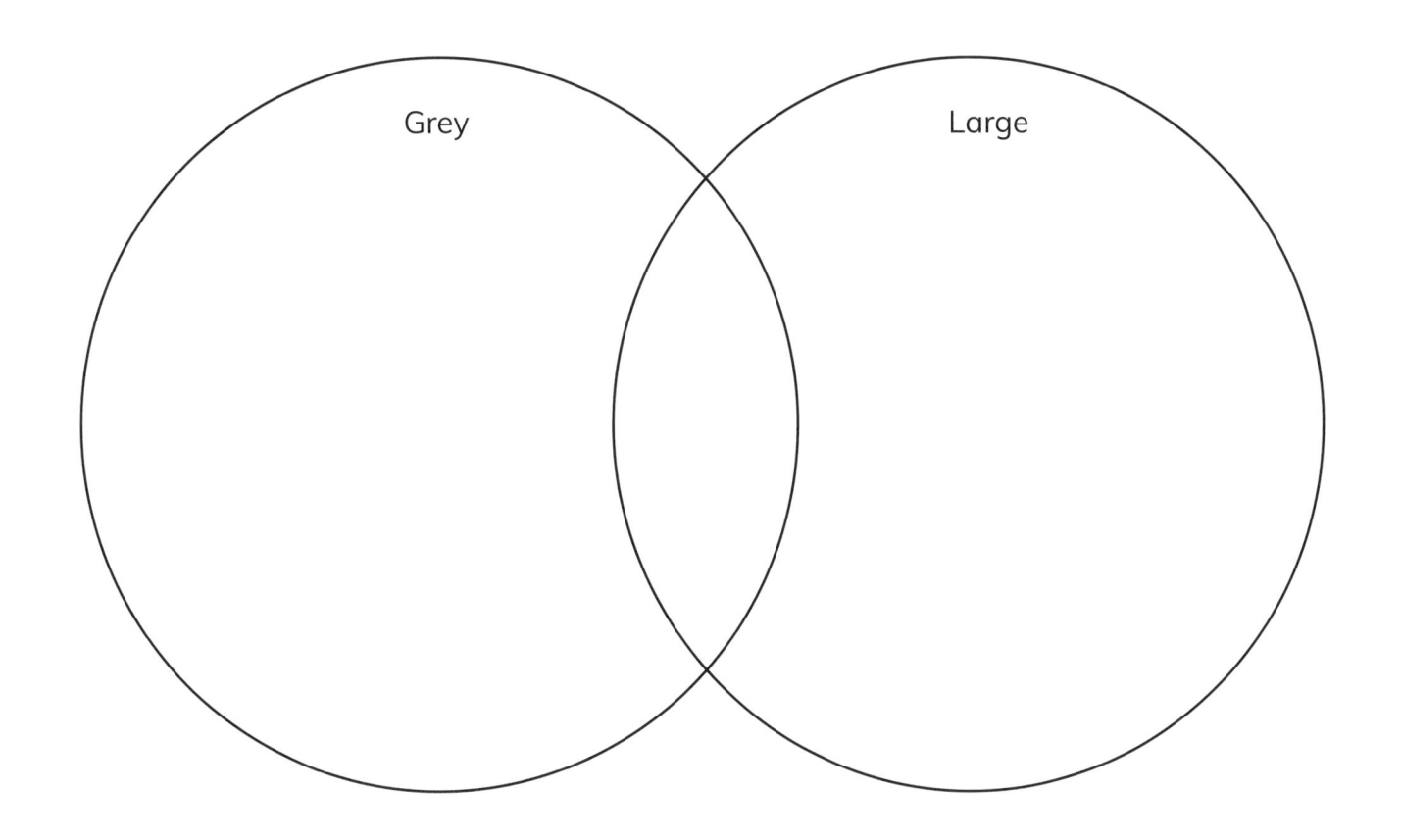

Grey              Large

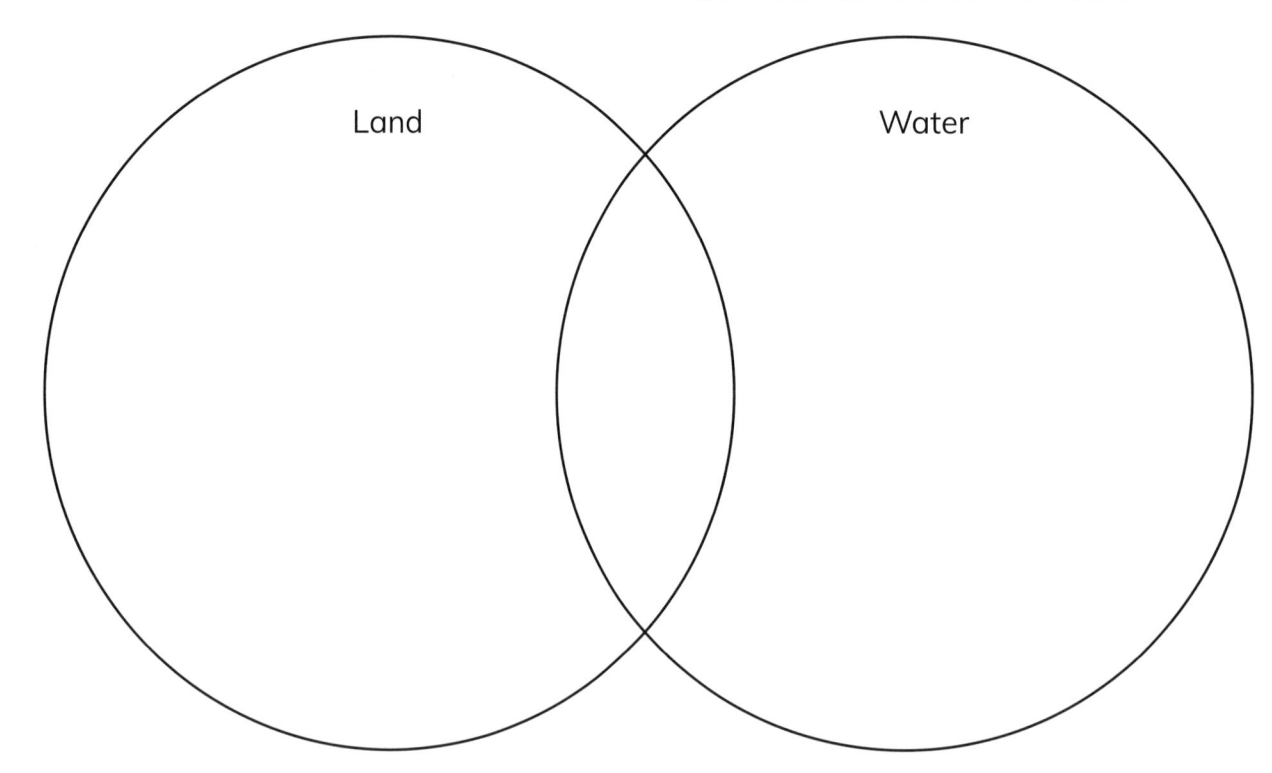

# 9 Statistics (2)

8 Make a list of land-living and water-living animals.

Have up to 12 in your list.

Write them on the Venn diagram.

1 _____   2 _____

3 _____   4 _____

5 _____   6 _____

7 _____   8 _____

9 _____   10 _____

11 _____   12 _____

Land         Water

9.1 Venn diagrams, lists and tables

9  Marcus asks 100 parents from his school whether they like milk or sugar in their coffee.

This Venn diagram shows his results.

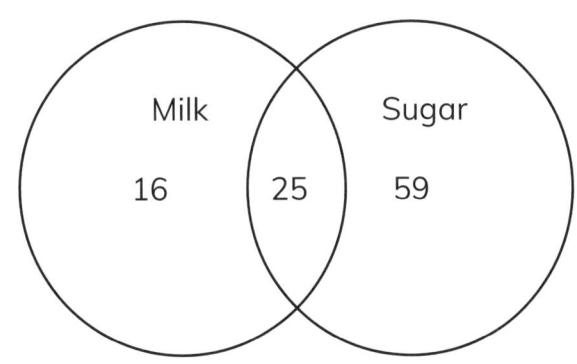

Milk  Sugar
16  25  59

How many like:

Milk ☐    Sugar ☐

Sugar but not milk ☐    Milk but not sugar ☐

Milk and sugar ☐    Milk or sugar ☐

Use the table below to show the same information.

|  |  |
|---|---|
|  |  |
|  |  |
|  |  |
|  |  |
|  |  |

143

# 9 Statistics (2)

## > 9.2 Pictograms and block graphs

### Exercise 9.2

**Focus**

> **Worked example 2**
>
> This pictogram shows the number of pizza slices eaten by a class in the school canteen.
>
> | | | | | | | |
> |---|---|---|---|---|---|---|
> | Monday | 🍕 | 🍕 | 🍕 | 🍕 | 🍕 | 🍕 |
> | Tuesday | 🍕 | 🍕 | 🍕 | 🍕 | | |
> | Wednesday | 🍕 | | | | | |
> | Thursday | 🍕 | 🍕 | 🍕 | | | |
>
> 🍕 = 1 slice
>
> What can you find out using the data in the pictogram?
>
> *If I count the slices, I know how many were eaten. I can count 14.*
>
> *I can find out which day most pizza was eaten. And which day only 1 piece was eaten.*
>
> *And I can find out how many were eaten on each day.*

9.2 Pictograms and block graphs

1. This pictogram shows the number of ice creams eaten on Thursday.

| Vanilla | 🍦 | 🍦 | 🍦 | 🍦 | 🍦 | | | |
|---|---|---|---|---|---|---|---|---|
| Chocolate | 🍦 | 🍦 | 🍦 | 🍦 | 🍦 | 🍦 | | |
| Strawberry | 🍦 | 🍦 | 🍦 | 🍦 | | | | |
| Coffee | 🍦 | | | | | | | |

🍦 = 1 ice cream

Which flavour was the most popular? _____

Which flavour was the least popular? _____

How many ice creams were eaten on Thursday? ☐

9 Statistics (2)

2  This block graph shows the goals scored so far this season.

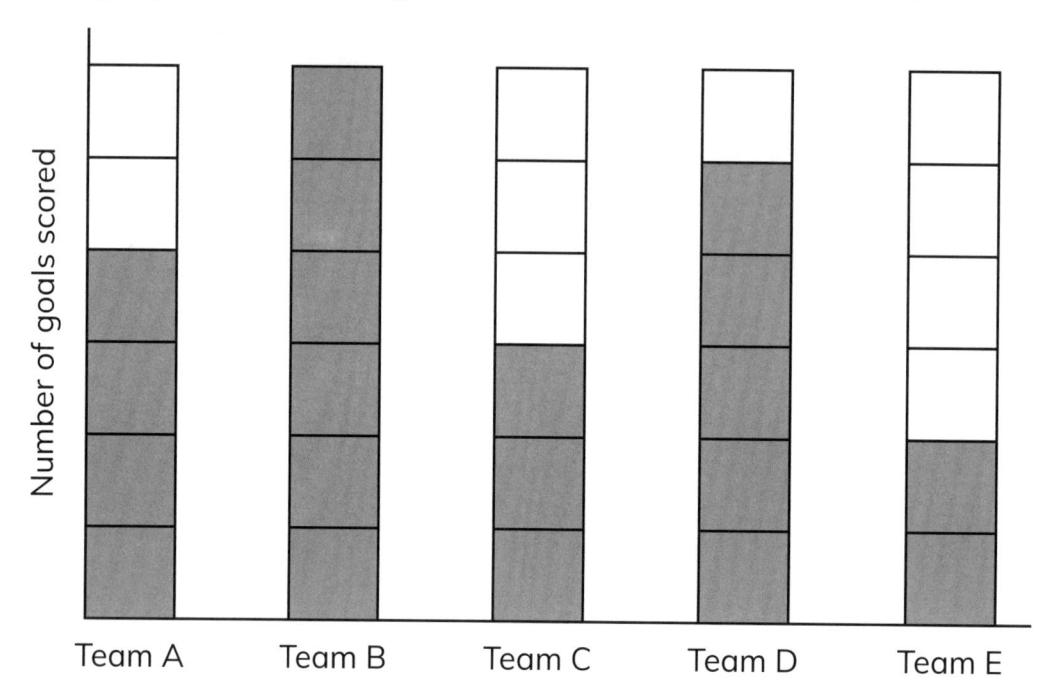

Number of goals scored

Team A    Team B    Team C    Team D    Team E

Which team has scored most goals? _____

Which team has scored the least goals? _____

How many more goals have been scored by Team B

than by Team D? ☐

How many fewer goals have been scored by Team E

than by Team A? ☐

9.2 Pictograms and block graphs

## Practice

3  This pictogram shows drinks that children in a class like.

| Water | 🍶 | 🍶 | | | |
|---|---|---|---|---|---|
| Orange juice | 🧃 | 🧃 | 🧃 | 🧃 | 🧃 |
| Milk | 🥛 | 🥛 | 🥛 | 🥛 | |
| Cola | 🥤 | 🥤 | 🥤 | | |
| Tea | ☕ | ☕ | | | |

1 picture = 1 child

How many children like orange juice? ☐

How many children like water? ☐

Which drink is liked by 3 children? _____

How many more children like milk than tea? ☐

How many children are asked altogether? ☐

Which is your favourite drink? _____

147

## 9 Statistics (2)

4  This block graph shows how many letters there are in some children's family names.

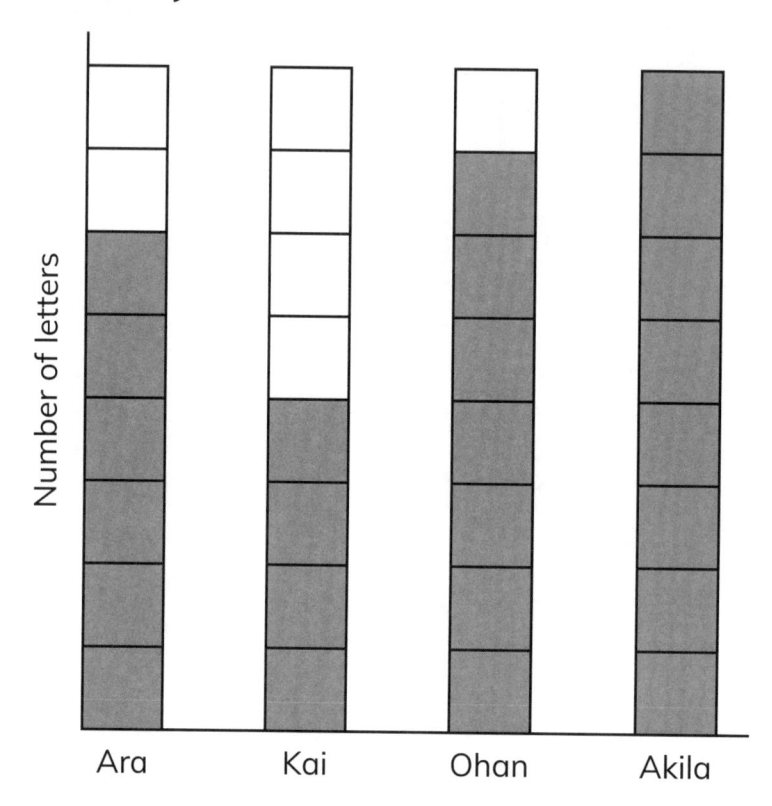

How many letters are in:

Ara's family name? ☐

Ohan's family name? ☐

Akila's family name? ☐

Whose family name has most letters? _____

Whose family name has least letters? _____

9.2 Pictograms and block graphs

How many more letters are in Ohan's family name than in Kai's family name? ☐

How many fewer letters are in Aria's family name than in Akila's family name? ☐

Write 2 more questions of your own.

1 _____

2 _____

## 9 Statistics (2)

**Challenge**

5 The pictogram shows fruit in a fruit bowl.

| Apples | 🍎 | 🍎 | 🍎 | 🍎 | 🍎 | 🍎 | 🍎 | | |
| --- | --- | --- | --- | --- | --- | --- | --- | --- | --- |
| Pears | 🍐 | 🍐 | 🍐 | 🍐 | | | | | |
| Kiwis | 🥝 | 🥝 | 🥝 | 🥝 | 🥝 | | | | |
| Mangoes | 🥭 | 🥭 | 🥭 | | | | | | |
| Oranges | 🍊 | 🍊 | 🍊 | 🍊 | | | | | |
| Bananas | 🍌 | 🍌 | 🍌 | 🍌 | 🍌 | 🍌 | | | |

1 picture = 1 piece of fruit

How many pieces of fruit are in the bowl? ☐

How many more pears are there than mangoes? ☐

How many fewer bananas are there than apples? ☐

Which are there most of in the bowl? _____

Which are there least of in the bowl? _____

Make a fruit salad. You can use 6 pieces of fruit.
What would you choose?

_____

6  Here are 5 telephone numbers.

842 229902   024 771024   061 382517   245 027538   143 195035

Find out how many times each of the digits 0 1 2 3 4 5 6 7 8 9 are used.

Complete the block graph to show your results.

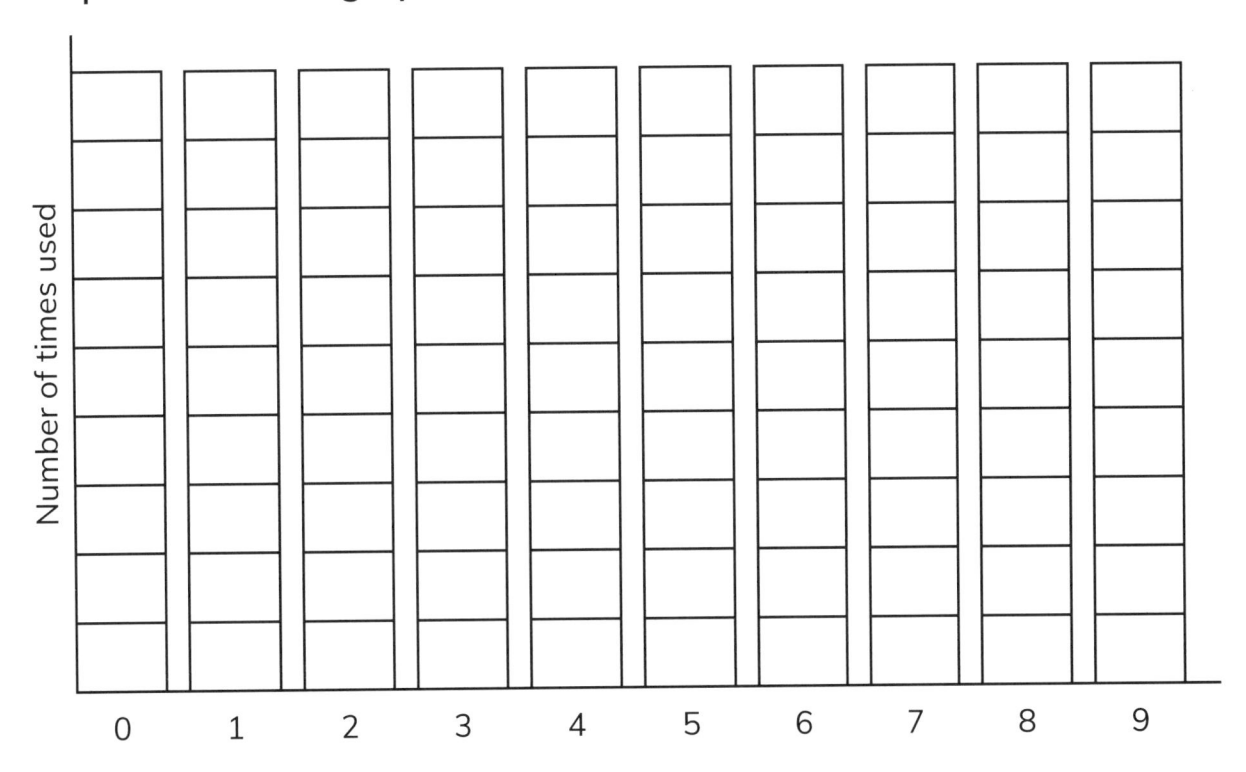

Number of times used

0   1   2   3   4   5   6   7   8   9

Write 4 questions using the data in this block graph.

1 _____

2 _____

3 _____

4 _____

# 10 Calculating

## > 10.1 Adding and subtracting two 2-digit numbers

Exercise 10.1

swap   total

**Focus**

1   Add two 2-digit numbers.

   a   32 + 26          b   41 + 35          c   23 + 34
       =                    =                    =

   d      57            e      43            f      23
       + 21                 + 14                 + 24

2   Solve each number sentence. Show your steps.

   | 10s | 1s |
   |---|---|
   | 🫘🫘🫘 | 🫛🫛🫛🫛 🫛🫛🫛🫛 |

   38 − 25 =

152

10.1 Adding and subtracting two 2-digit numbers

| 10s | 1s |
|---|---|
| ●  ●<br>●  ● | ○ ○ ○<br>○ ○ ○ |

46 − 12 =

3   Use the 100 square to help you find the totals.

a   27 + 12 = ☐

b   33 + 24 = ☐

| 1 | 2 | 3 | 4 | 5 | 6 | 7 | 8 | 9 | 10 |
|---|---|---|---|---|---|---|---|---|---|
| 11 | 12 | 13 | 14 | 15 | 16 | 17 | 18 | 19 | 20 |
| 21 | 22 | 23 | 24 | 25 | 26 | 27 | 28 | 29 | 30 |
| 31 | 32 | 33 | 34 | 35 | 36 | 37 | 38 | 39 | 40 |
| 41 | 42 | 43 | 44 | 45 | 46 | 47 | 48 | 49 | 50 |
| 51 | 52 | 53 | 54 | 55 | 56 | 57 | 58 | 59 | 60 |
| 61 | 62 | 63 | 64 | 65 | 66 | 67 | 68 | 69 | 70 |
| 71 | 72 | 73 | 74 | 75 | 76 | 77 | 78 | 79 | 80 |
| 81 | 82 | 83 | 84 | 85 | 86 | 87 | 88 | 89 | 90 |
| 91 | 92 | 93 | 94 | 95 | 96 | 97 | 98 | 99 | 100 |

# 10 Calculating

## Worked example 1

Find the difference between 26 and 38.

Show both numbers on a 100 square or number line.

| 1 | 2 | 3 | 4 | 5 | 6 | 7 | 8 | 9 | 10 |
|---|---|---|---|---|---|---|---|---|---|
| 11 | 12 | 13 | 14 | 15 | 16 | 17 | 18 | 19 | 20 |
| 21 | 22 | 23 | 24 | 25 | 26 | 27 | 28 | 29 | 30 |
| 31 | 32 | 33 | 34 | 35 | 36 | 37 | 38 | 39 | 40 |
| 41 | 42 | 43 | 44 | 45 | 46 | 47 | 48 | 49 | 50 |
| 51 | 52 | 53 | 54 | 55 | 56 | 57 | 58 | 59 | 60 |
| 61 | 62 | 63 | 64 | 65 | 66 | 67 | 68 | 69 | 70 |
| 71 | 72 | 73 | 74 | 75 | 76 | 77 | 78 | 79 | 80 |
| 81 | 82 | 83 | 84 | 85 | 86 | 87 | 88 | 89 | 90 |
| 91 | 92 | 93 | 94 | 95 | 96 | 97 | 98 | 99 | 100 |

Count on from 26 to 38.

I counted on ten to 36. Then I counted on in ones to 37 then 38. That's 12. The difference between 26 and 38 is 12.

Answer: 38 − 26 = 12

10.1 Adding and subtracting two 2-digit numbers

4   Find the difference between each pair of numbers.

Write the number sentence. Use the 100 square to help you.

21  34        46  67

| 1 | 2 | 3 | 4 | 5 | 6 | 7 | 8 | 9 | 10 |
|---|---|---|---|---|---|---|---|---|----|
| 11 | 12 | 13 | 14 | 15 | 16 | 17 | 18 | 19 | 20 |
| 21 | 22 | 23 | 24 | 25 | 26 | 27 | 28 | 29 | 30 |
| 31 | 32 | 33 | 34 | 35 | 36 | 37 | 38 | 39 | 40 |
| 41 | 42 | 43 | 44 | 45 | 46 | 47 | 48 | 49 | 50 |
| 51 | 52 | 53 | 54 | 55 | 56 | 57 | 58 | 59 | 60 |
| 61 | 62 | 63 | 64 | 65 | 66 | 67 | 68 | 69 | 70 |
| 71 | 72 | 73 | 74 | 75 | 76 | 77 | 78 | 79 | 80 |
| 81 | 82 | 83 | 84 | 85 | 86 | 87 | 88 | 89 | 90 |
| 91 | 92 | 93 | 94 | 95 | 96 | 97 | 98 | 99 | 100 |

## 10 Calculating

**Practice**

5 Choose a number from each cloud to add together. Do this 3 times. Write your number sentences. Which method will you use?

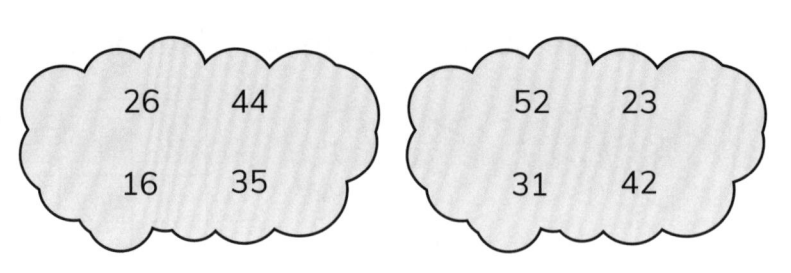

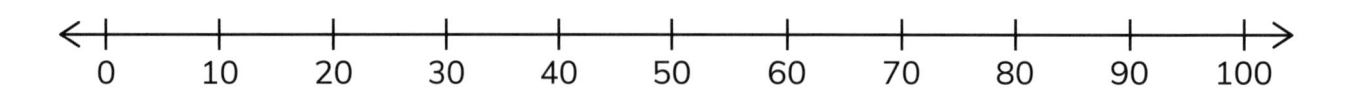

Cloud 1: 26, 44, 16, 35
Cloud 2: 52, 23, 31, 42

Number line: 0, 10, 20, 30, 40, 50, 60, 70, 80, 90, 100

| 10s | 1s |
|---|---|
|  |  |

_____

_____

_____

6 Complete the grid. Which methods will you use to find the missing numbers?

| 42 |  |  |
|---|---|---|
|  |  |  |
|  |  |  |

−26 ←

| 68 | 47 | 79 |
|---|---|---|
| 57 | 89 | 97 |
| 49 | 87 | 58 |

156

## 10.1 Adding and subtracting two 2-digit numbers

7 Marcus makes some mistakes when he writes these number facts.

Tick those that are correct.

Correct any that are not equivalent in value.

53 + 24 = 54 + 25          63 + 25 = 53 + 35

85 − 33 = 95 − 23          37 − 12 = 39 − 14

8 The difference between two numbers is 23.

If one of the numbers is 74, what could the other number be?

## Challenge

9 Using the digits 1, 2, 3, 4 and 5 only once, make two 2-digit numbers. Add the two numbers together.

What is the smallest total you can make?

What is the greatest total you can make?

## 10 Calculating

10 Complete this number puzzle.

**Clues**

Across

1. 42 + 33
3. 99 − 42
5. 18 + 21
8. 79 − 31
10. 85 − 22
12. 88 − 14
14. 79 − 55

Down

2. 87 − 34
4. 97 − 26
6. 51 + 43
7. 88 − 22
9. 44 + 43
11. 77 − 45
13. 84 − 43

# 10.2 Connecting addition and subtraction

Exercise 10.2

fact family   inverse

**Focus**

1   Find an inverse calculation for each calculation in the table.

| Calculation | Inverse |
|---|---|
| 7 + 3 = 10 | |
| 13 + 5 = 18 | |
| 32 + 17 = 49 | |
| 8 − 6 = 2 | |
| 19 − 12 = 7 | |
| 28 − 15 = 13 | |

2   Write two different additions with a total of 20.

   Find an inverse calculation for each addition.

## 10 Calculating

**Worked example 2**

Write the fact family for this representation.

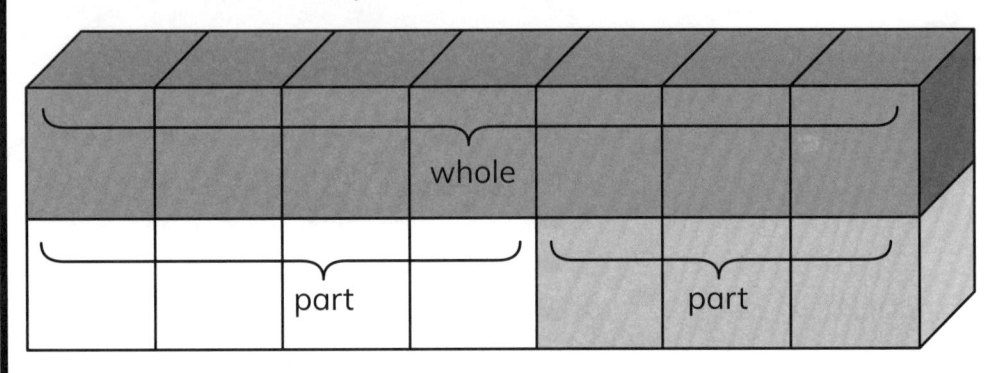

[bar model showing whole of 7 split into parts of 4 and 3]

4 + 3 = 7   7 = 4 + 3
3 + 4 = 7   7 = 3 + 4

7 − 4 = 3   3 = 7 − 4
7 − 3 = 4   4 = 7 − 3

> You can add in any order. Each addition can be written starting with the total. That's half the fact family.

> 7 is the total, first I can subtract 4. Then I can subtract 3. Each subtraction can be written starting with the answer. That's the other half of the fact family.

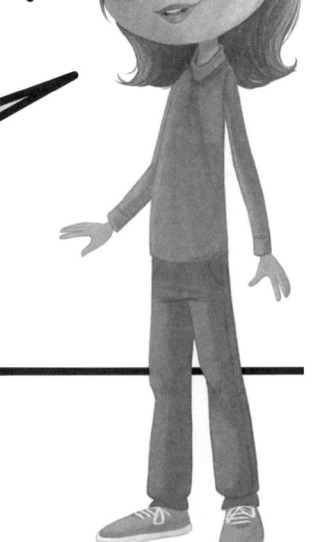

10.2 Connecting addition and subtraction

3   Write the fact family for this representation.

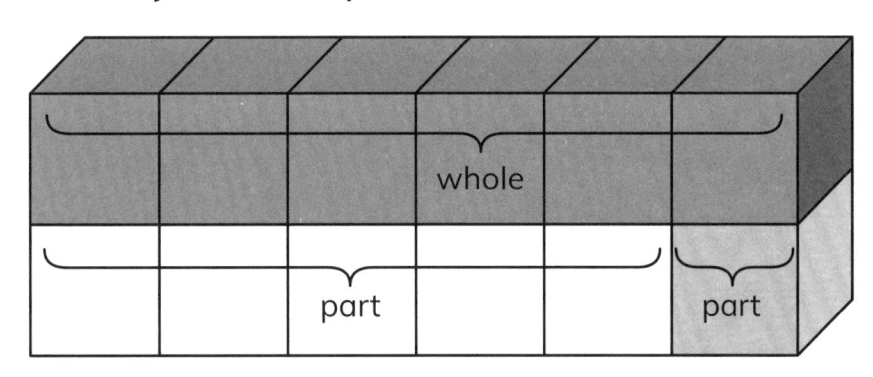

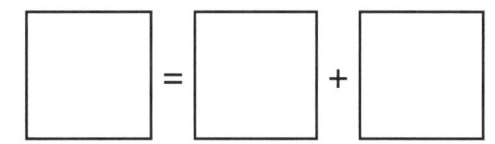

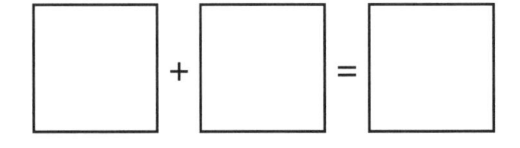

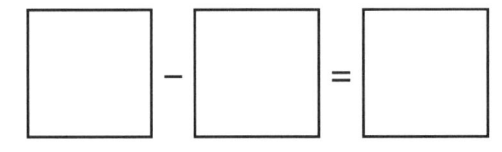

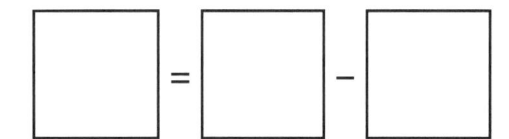

☐ + ☐ = ☐          ☐ = ☐ + ☐

☐ + ☐ = ☐          ☐ = ☐ + ☐

☐ − ☐ = ☐          ☐ = ☐ − ☐

☐ − ☐ = ☐          ☐ = ☐ − ☐

# 10 Calculating

## Practice

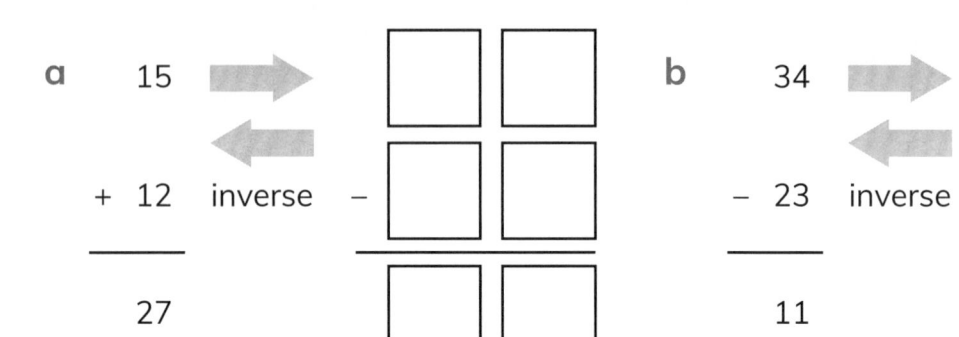

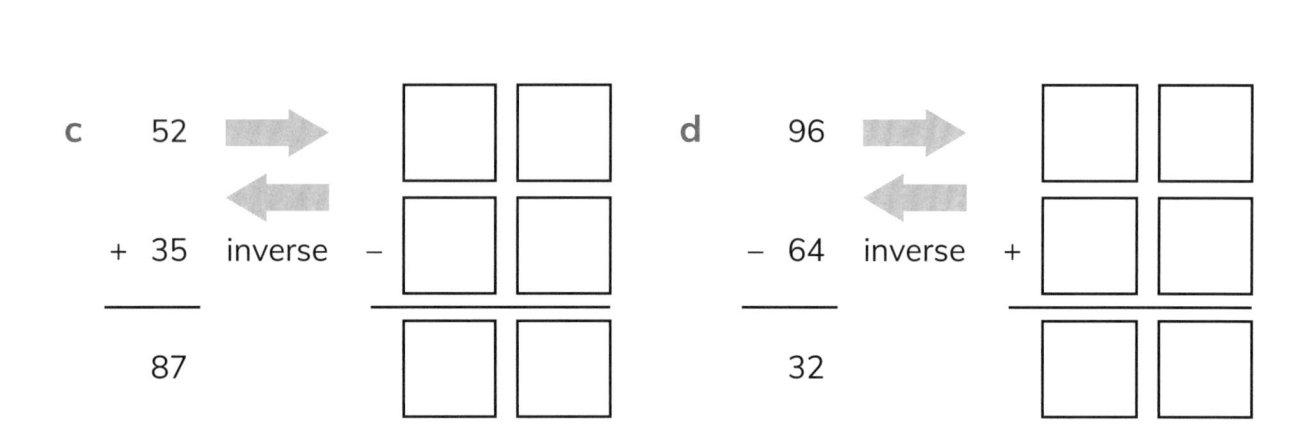

4 Find an inverse calculation to check each calculation.

a)
```
   15  →
       ←
 + 12    inverse   –
 ____              ____
   27
```

b)
```
   34  →
       ←
 – 23    inverse   +
 ____              ____
   11
```

c)
```
   52  →
       ←
 + 35    inverse   –
 ____              ____
   87
```

d)
```
   96  →
       ←
 – 64    inverse   +
 ____              ____
   32
```

10.2 Connecting addition and subtraction

5  Find the missing digit in each calculation.

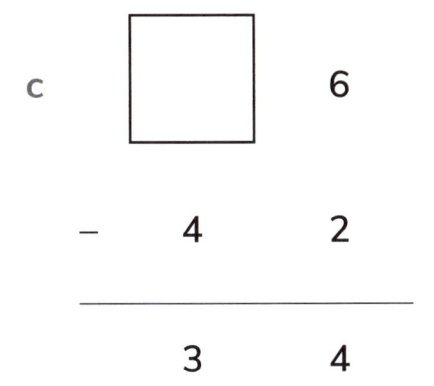

a
```
   ☐ 3
 + 2 4
 ─────
   5 7
```

b
```
   4 9
 - 2 ☐
 ─────
   2 2
```

c
```
   ☐ 6
 - 4 2
 ─────
   3 4
```

d
```
   6 5
 + 1 ☐
 ─────
   7 9
```

Discuss how to find the missing digit with your partner or carer.

## 10 Calculating

6  Complete each fact family house.

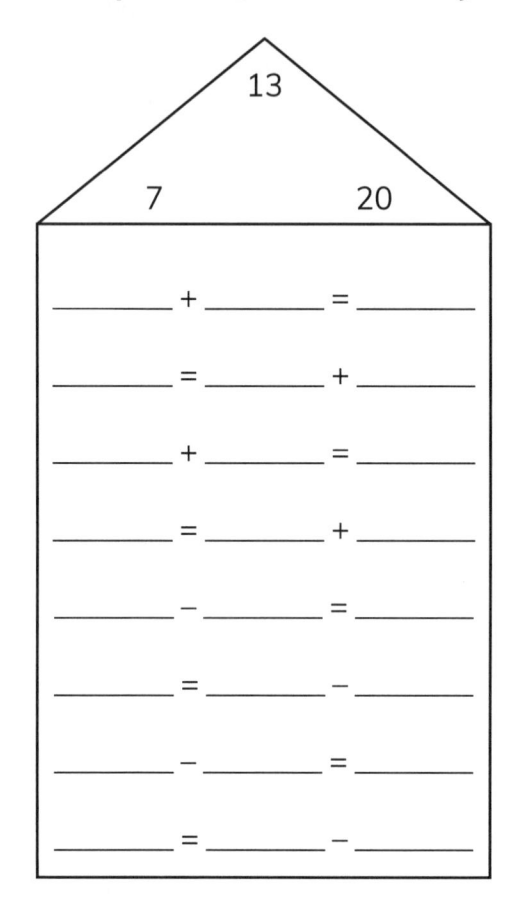

```
        /\                                    /\
       /13\                                  /15\
      /____\                                /____\
   7 /      \ 20                        13 /      \ 28
    /_____\                            /_____\
   |          |                          |          |
   |  ___ + ___ = ___                   |  ___ + ___ = ___
   |                                    |
   |  ___ = ___ + ___                   |  ___ = ___ + ___
   |                                    |
   |  ___ + ___ = ___                   |  ___ + ___ = ___
   |                                    |
   |  ___ = ___ + ___                   |  ___ = ___ + ___
   |                                    |
   |  ___ − ___ = ___                   |  ___ − ___ = ___
   |                                    |
   |  ___ = ___ − ___                   |  ___ = ___ − ___
   |                                    |
   |  ___ − ___ = ___                   |  ___ − ___ = ___
   |                                    |
   |  ___ = ___ − ___                   |  ___ = ___ − ___
   |_____|                          |_____|
```

7  The number sentence 50 + 40 = 90 shows two complements of 90.

   Write the 4 related subtraction calculations from the fact family.

8  Estimate, solve and use an inverse calculation to check.

   a  54 + 35         b  77 − 44

**Tip**

Round each number to the nearest 10 to help you estimate your answer.

# Challenge

9  Find the missing digits in each calculation.

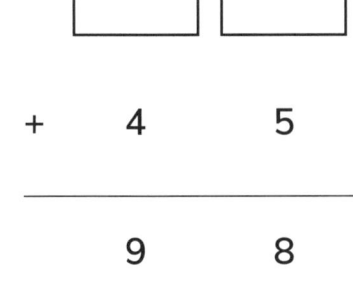

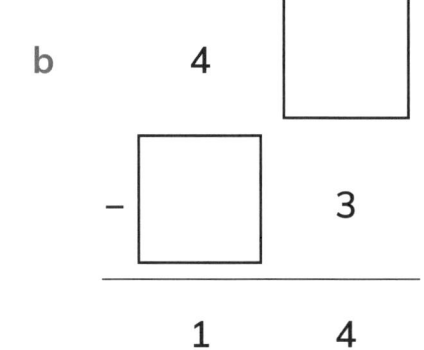

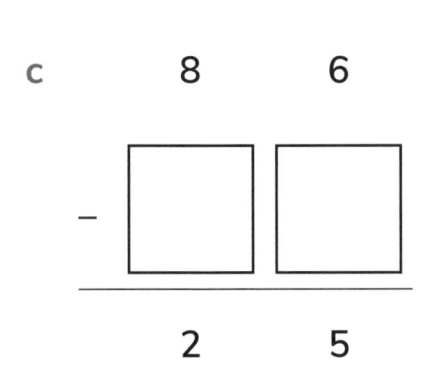

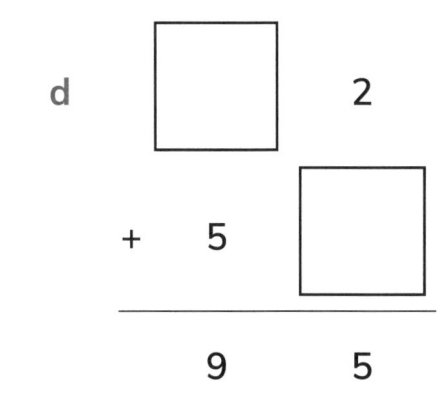

a)  
     5 3  
+  4 5  
─────  
  9 8

b)  
  4 7  
−  3 3  
─────  
  1 4

c)  
  8 6  
−  6 1  
─────  
  2 5

d)  
  4 2  
+  5 3  
─────  
  9 5

10  The number sentence 30 + 30 = 60 shows two complements of 60.

Why are there only 2 related subtractions in the fact family for this calculation?

_____

_____

_____

## 10 Calculating

11  Marcus rounds two numbers to the nearest 10 to estimate the total of his addition, 40 + 30 = 70. The answer to his addition is 74.

What could Marcus's addition have been?

Find all the possible solutions.

Check each addition using an inverse calculation.

12  Zara rounds her numbers to the nearest 10 to estimate the answer to her subtraction, 70 − 40 = 30. The answer to her subtraction is 27.

What could Zara's subtraction have been?

Find all the possible solutions.

Check each subtraction using an inverse calculation.

# 10.3 Multiplication

Exercise 10.3

product

**Focus**

1  Write the multiplication sentences.
   The first one has been done for you.

   Half of: 10 × 8 = 80 → $5 × 8 = 40$

   Double: 5 × 4 = 20 → _____

   Half of: 10 × 3 = 30 → _____

   Double: 5 × 9 = 45 → _____

2  Use the connection between doubling and multiplying by 2 to find the missing facts.

| Multiplying by 2 | Doubling |
|---|---|
| 1 × 2 = 2 |  |
|  | 10 + 10 = 20 |
| 2 × 2 = 4 |  |
|  | 5 + 5 = 10 |

## 10 Calculating

**3** The equal product machine makes equivalent multiplication calculations.

Look at the calculations going into the machine.

What calculations might come out of the machine?

10 × 1 = 10

2 × 10 = 20

4 × 2 = 8

Write your three equivalent facts.

☐ × ☐ = ☐ × ☐

☐ × ☐ = ☐ × ☐

☐ × ☐ = ☐ × ☐

**4** Which pair of equivalent multiplication facts do these cubes represent?

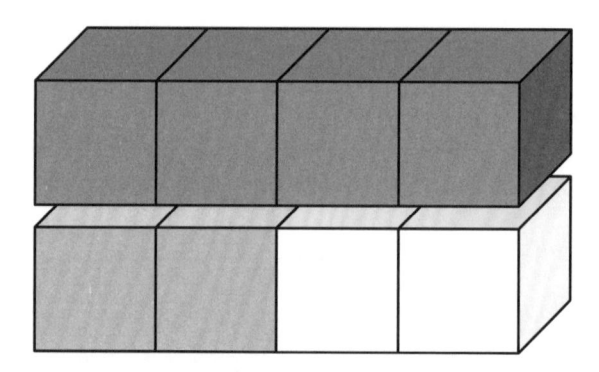

10.3 Multiplication

## Practice

5  Sofia uses 10 hands to make two different multiplication facts from the multiplication table for 5. What could those facts be?

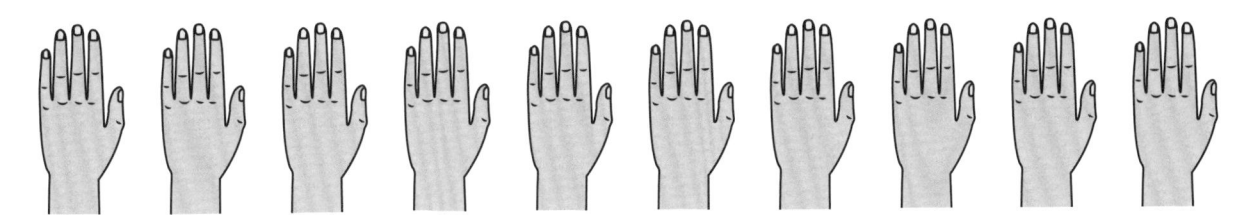

_____

_____

Zara uses five pairs of hands to make two different multiplication facts for the multiplication table for 10. What could those facts be?

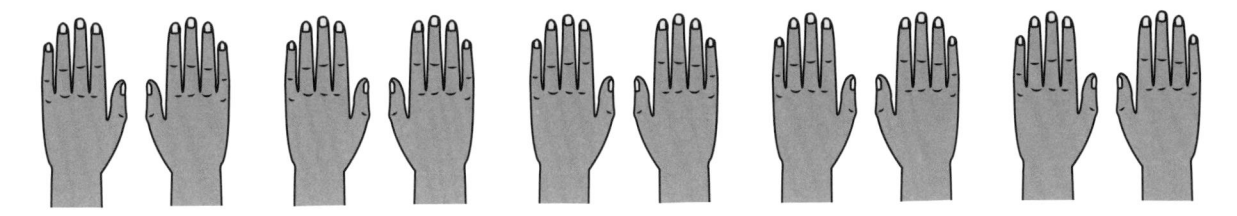

_____

_____

6  Draw lines to connect the equivalent calculations.

3 × 2          10 + 10

10 × 2         6 + 6

1 × 2          3 + 3

6 × 2          1 + 1

## 10 Calculating

7 The teacher points to this place on the counting stick.
Which multiplication facts could this represent?

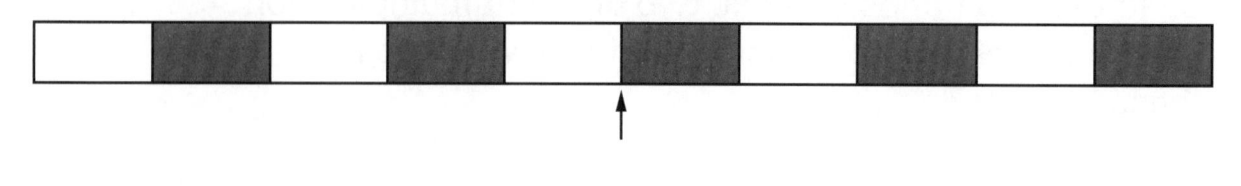

_____

_____

## Challenge

8 Which products are in both the multiplication table for 5 and the multiplication table for 10? Explain why.

_____

_____

9 Arun writes 10 × 4 = 40 to find the cost of 4 biscuits.

Is he correct?

Explain how you know.

Each

_____

_____

Sofia writes 10 × 7 = 70 to find the cost of 7 cakes.

Is she correct?

Explain how you know.

Each

_____

10 Put these statements in order of their value, from smallest to greatest.

10 × 5    5 × 3    2 × 6    1 × 7    5 × 4    10 × 3

# > 10.4 Division

Exercise 10.4

quotient

## Focus

1  Complete the multiplication table for 10.
   Use it to write the division facts for 10.

   10 × 1 = 10              10 ÷ 10 = 1

   10 × 2 = 20              _____

   10 × 3 =                 _____

   10 × 4 =                 _____

   _____          _____

   _____          _____

   _____          _____

   _____          _____

## 10 Calculating

2. Write the inverse division fact for each multiplication fact.

   $2 \times 3 = 6$ _____

   $1 \times 5 = 5$ _____

   $5 \times 7 = 35$ _____

3. Write a division fact with the same value as the multiplication fact.

   $5 \times 2 = $ _____

   $9 \times 1 = $ _____

## Practice

4. Write a multiplication fact and the inverse division fact for each picture.

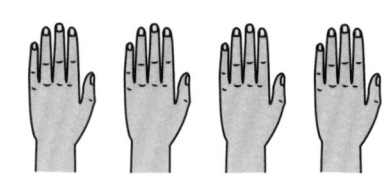

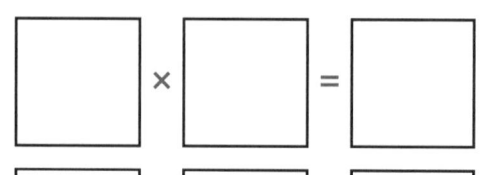

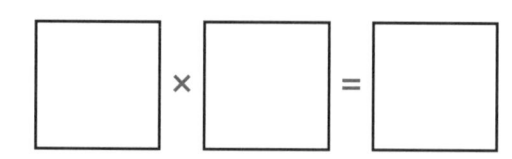

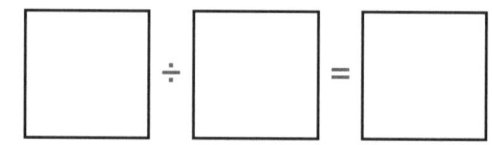

   ☐ × ☐ = ☐

   ☐ ÷ ☐ = ☐

   ☐ × ☐ = ☐

   ☐ ÷ ☐ = ☐

5   When a product and a quotient have the same value, the facts are equivalent in value.

Write three equivalent statements.

☐ × ☐ = ☐ ÷ ☐

☐ ÷ ☐ = ☐ × ☐

☐ × ☐ = ☐ ÷ ☐

Discuss how you found your answers with a partner or carer.

6   Write the matching division or fraction fact.

| Division fact | Fraction fact |
|---|---|
|  | $\frac{1}{2}$ of 18 = 9 |
| 14 ÷ 2 = 7 |  |
| 16 ÷ 4 = 4 |  |
|  | $\frac{1}{4}$ of 4 = 1 |

## 10 Calculating

## Challenge

7  Marcus makes a cube snake using 16 cubes.

Zara's snake uses half as many cubes as Marcus. Arun's snake uses only a quarter of the cubes that Marcus' snake uses.

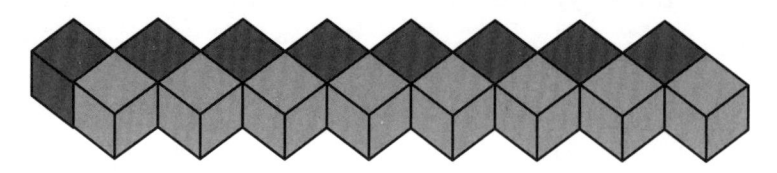

How many cubes are there in Zara's snake?
Write two number sentences to show how you found out.

How many cubes are there in Arun's snake?
Write two number sentences to show how you found out.

8  Put these calculations in order of their value, from smallest to greatest.

18 ÷ 2        6 × 2        40 ÷ 10        $\frac{1}{2}$ of 12        $\frac{1}{4}$ of 20

9  Arun writes a set of 4 equivalent calculations for 1 × 8.
Starting with 1 × 8, can you write a set of equivalent calculations longer than Arun's?

# 11 Geometry (2)

## > 11.1 Angles and turns

**Worked example 1**

How can Sofia get home? Colour a route that she takes.

| angle |
| anticlockwise |
| clockwise |
| half turn |
| quarter turn |
| right angle |
| turn |
| full turn |

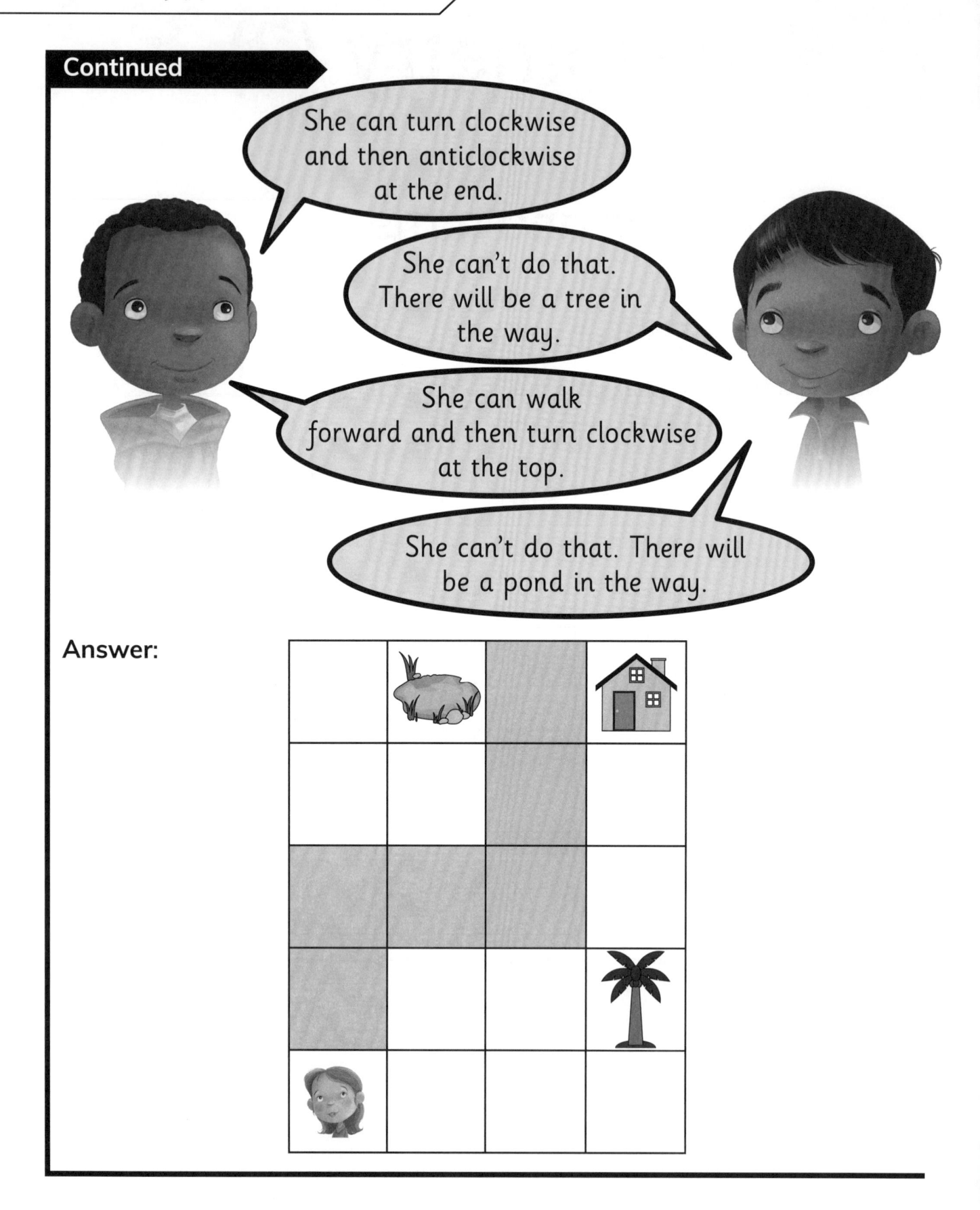

11  Geometry (2)

**Continued**

She can turn clockwise and then anticlockwise at the end.

She can't do that. There will be a tree in the way.

She can walk forward and then turn clockwise at the top.

She can't do that. There will be a pond in the way.

Answer:

# Exercise 11.1

## Focus

1 Follow the grey path and make a cross at every right angle quarter turn you make.

The first two have been done for you.

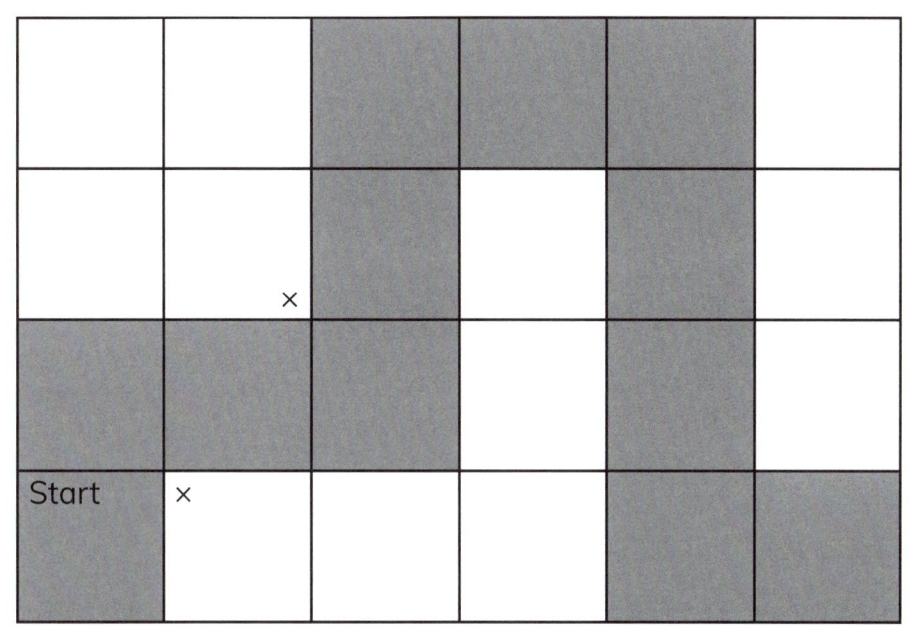

How many right angle turns do you make? ☐

How many anticlockwise turns? ☐

How many clockwise turns? ☐

## 11 Geometry (2)

2. Look for angles on your table. It may be a book, a pencil case or even the table.

   Draw what you can see.

   | What can you see? | Draw it |
   |---|---|
   |  |  |
   |  |  |
   |  |  |

3  Predict and check how many times these shapes look identical as they complete a full turn.

Complete the table.

| Shape | Predict | Check |
|---|---|---|
| ↑ | | |
| ◗ | | |
| ☐ | | |
| ▭ | | |

Draw a shape that will look identical 3 times as it completes a full turn.

## 11 Geometry (2)

**Practice**

4   Colour a path that has 5 right angle quarter turns.

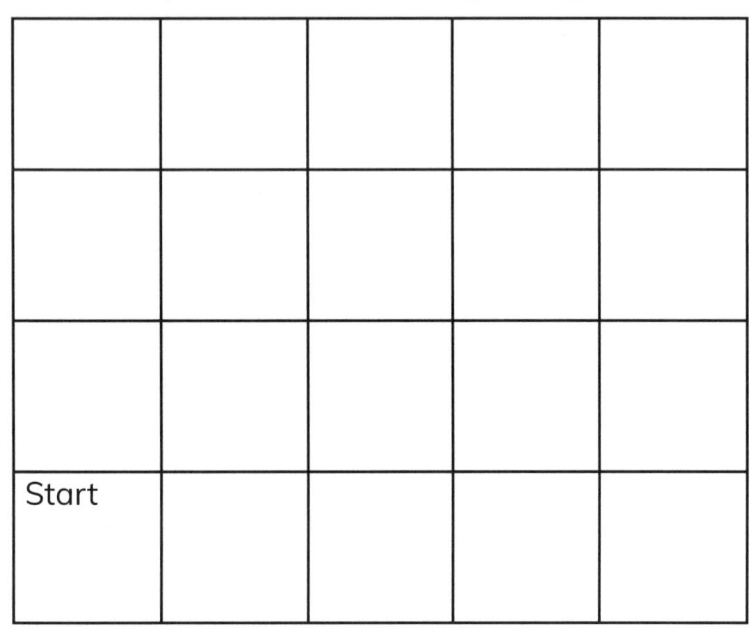

Show the turns with a cross ✗.

5   Shape A looks like this.

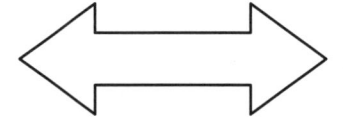

  a   Draw a ring around the shape that shows Shape A after half a turn.

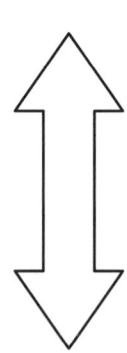

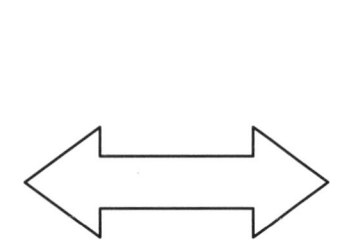

b   Draw a ring around the shape that shows
    Shape A after a full turn.

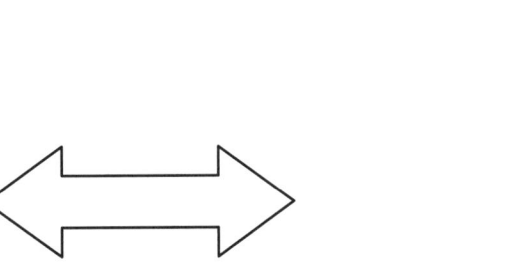

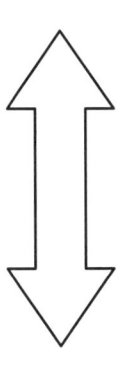

c   Draw a ring around the shape that shows
    Shape A after a quarter turn.

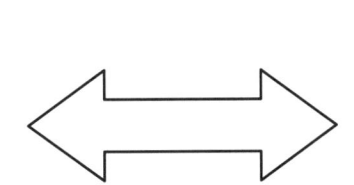

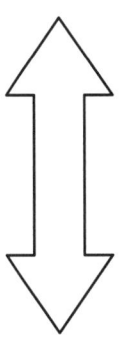

6   Look at these shapes.

    Draw what they would look like at the end of 3 half turns clockwise and anticlockwise.

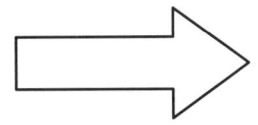

# 11 Geometry (2)

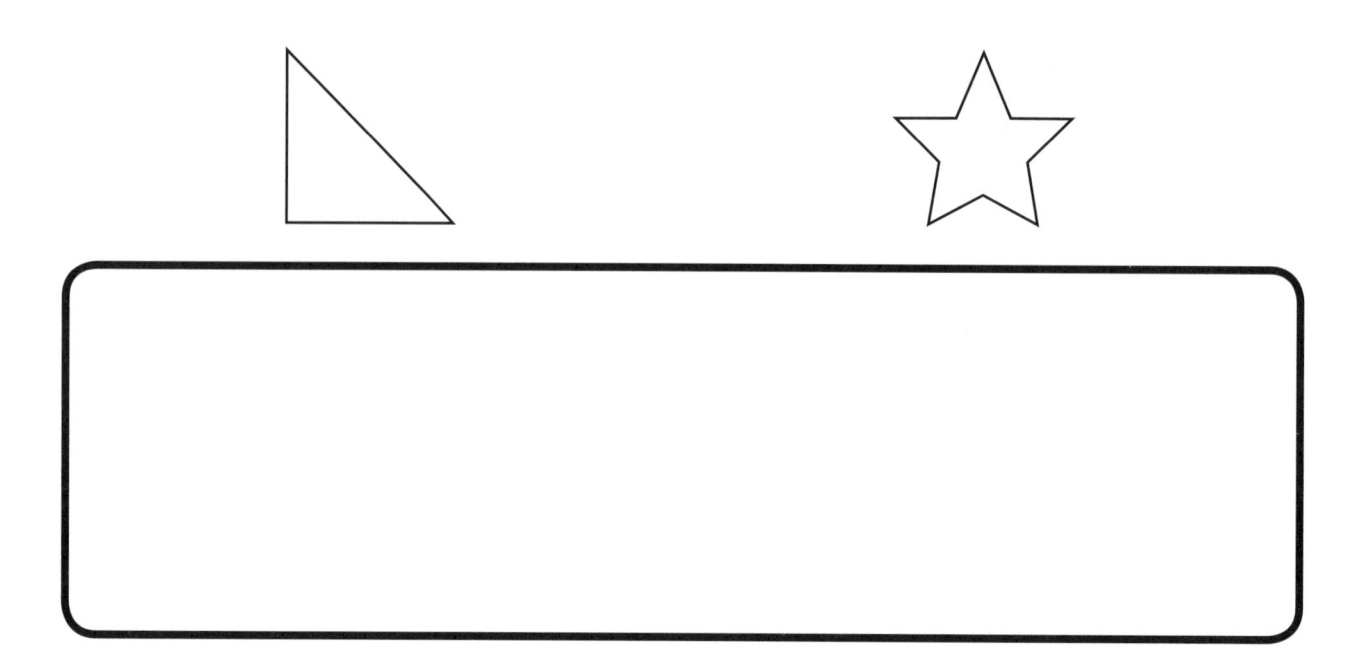

## Challenge

7. On a piece of paper, write the instructions to get the elephant to its house. Draw the path as you go.

   Use the words: clockwise, anticlockwise, quarter turn, half turn, full turn.

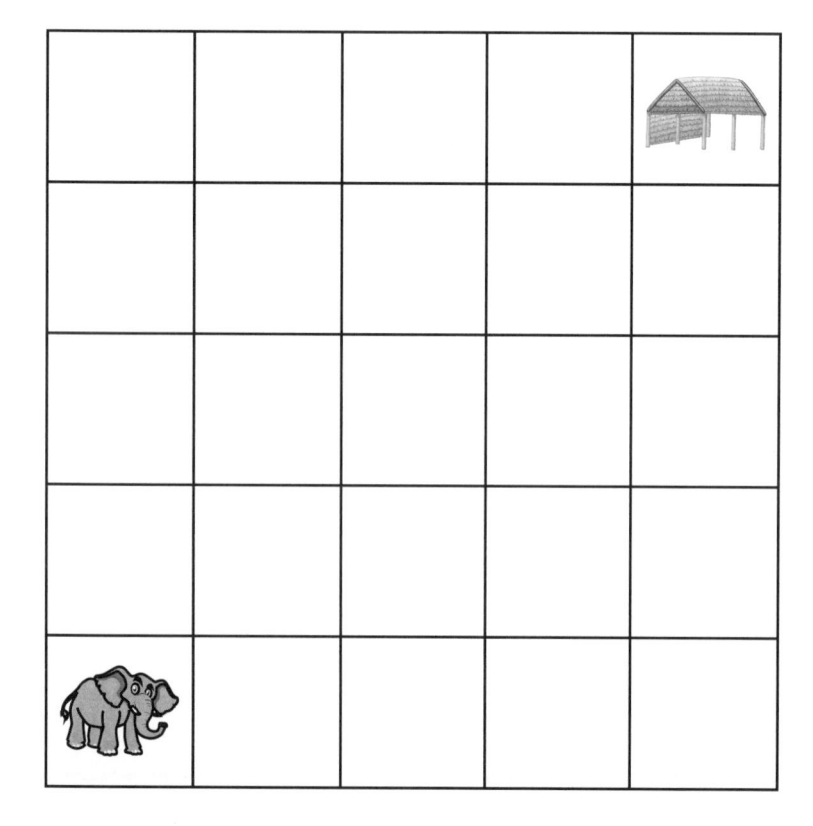

**Tip**

Remember the elephant has to face the way it is walking.

11.1 Angles and turns

8   Lyra the ladybird wants to see the spider.

She says, 'I can make a half turn clockwise or I can make two quarter turns anticlockwise.'

a   How else can Lyra turn to see the spider?
    Think of at least two ways.

    I can _____

    I can _____

b   Now Lyra is facing the spider, how can she turn to see the worm? Think of at least four ways.

    I can _____

    I can _____

    I can _____

    I can _____

183

# 11 Geometry (2)

9  Turn and draw the shapes a half turn clockwise.

Draw where the dots would be.

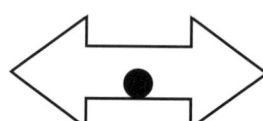

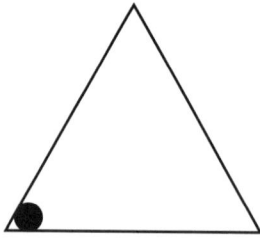

184

# > 11.2 Circles

## Exercise 11.2

### Focus

centre   distance

1   Use a ruler.

Which circle shows the centre dot?

Draw 4 lines from the centre dot of that circle to the edge.

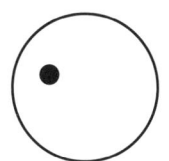

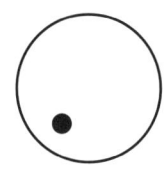

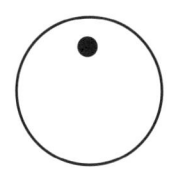

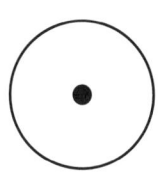

Measure the lines you drew.

How long is each line?  _____

Tell a parent or carer what you notice about the length of these lines.

### Practice

2   The distance from one edge to the other through the centre point is written under each circle.

*The drawings are not accurate, so do not measure them to get your answer.*

How long would one line from the centre to an edge be?
Write your answer below each circle.

Show the centre point and draw the line on each circle.

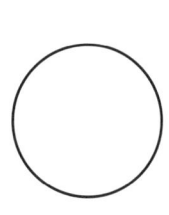

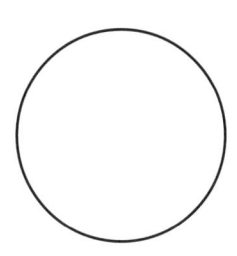

8 centimetres          10 centimetres          12 centimetres

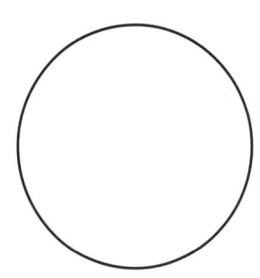

_____          _____          _____

# 11 Geometry (2)

## Challenge

3   Use a ruler.

Join 4 sets of numbers to find the centre of the clock.

The numbers in each set must be opposite each other on the clock. The first one has been done for you.

How many lines did you draw? ☐

How many lines come from the centre to the edge? ☐

Are they all the same length? Measure them.

They all measure _____ .

# 12 Telling the time

## > 12.1 Telling the time

Exercise 12.1

> analogue clock   digital clock
> quarter past   quarter to

**Focus**

1   Complete the digital clocks to match the analogue clocks.

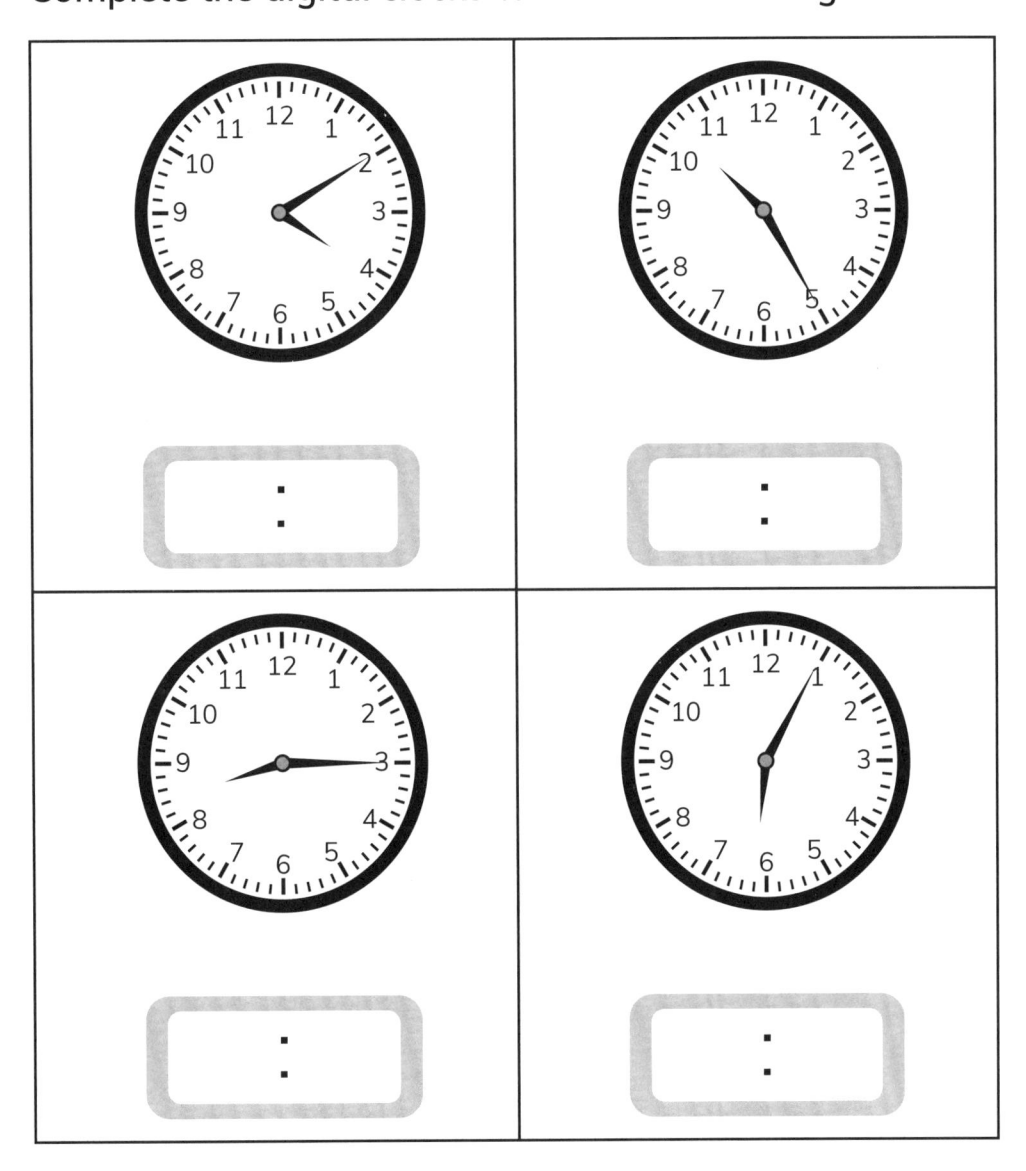

## 12 Telling the time

2   Draw the hands on the analogue clocks to match the digital clocks.

| 06:15 | 07:20 |
| 05:05 | 04:25 |

12.1 Telling the time

3   Make each pair of clocks show the same time.

| 07:55 | 10:35 |
| 08:45 | 09:30 |
| 01:40 | 07:33 |

## 12 Telling the time

4  How many minutes are there in quarter of an hour?

_____ minutes

## Practice

5  Make each pair of clocks show the given time.

| 25 minutes past 8 | 5 minutes to 12 | 15 minutes to 4 |
| --- | --- | --- |
| 25 minutes to 3 | 10 minutes past 10 | 20 minutes past 6 |

12.1 Telling the time

6   Complete the clocks. Draw a ring around the correct time of day.

| Quarter past 9 | Good morning! | Morning / Afternoon / Evening |
| Quarter to 7 | Can I watch TV before I go to bed? | Morning / Afternoon / Evening |
| Quarter to 4 | Welcome to after-school club | Morning / Afternoon / Evening |

## 12 Telling the time

## Challenge

7   Spin the spinner to choose the hour, spin again to choose how many sets of 5 minutes past the hour. Record the time on the clocks and in words. Repeat.

Here are some words to help you: minutes, to, past, quarter, half.

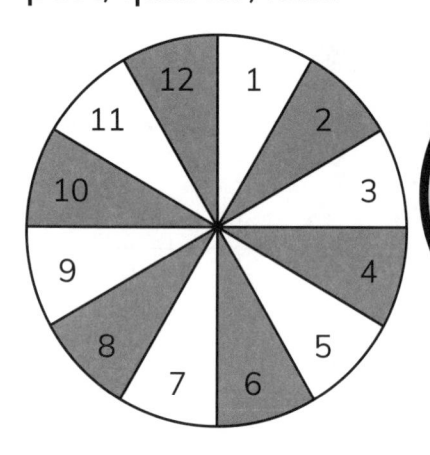

**Tip**

My spin for the hour was 3. My spin for the minutes was 7, so that is 35 minutes past the hour because 5 × 7 = 35.

03:35

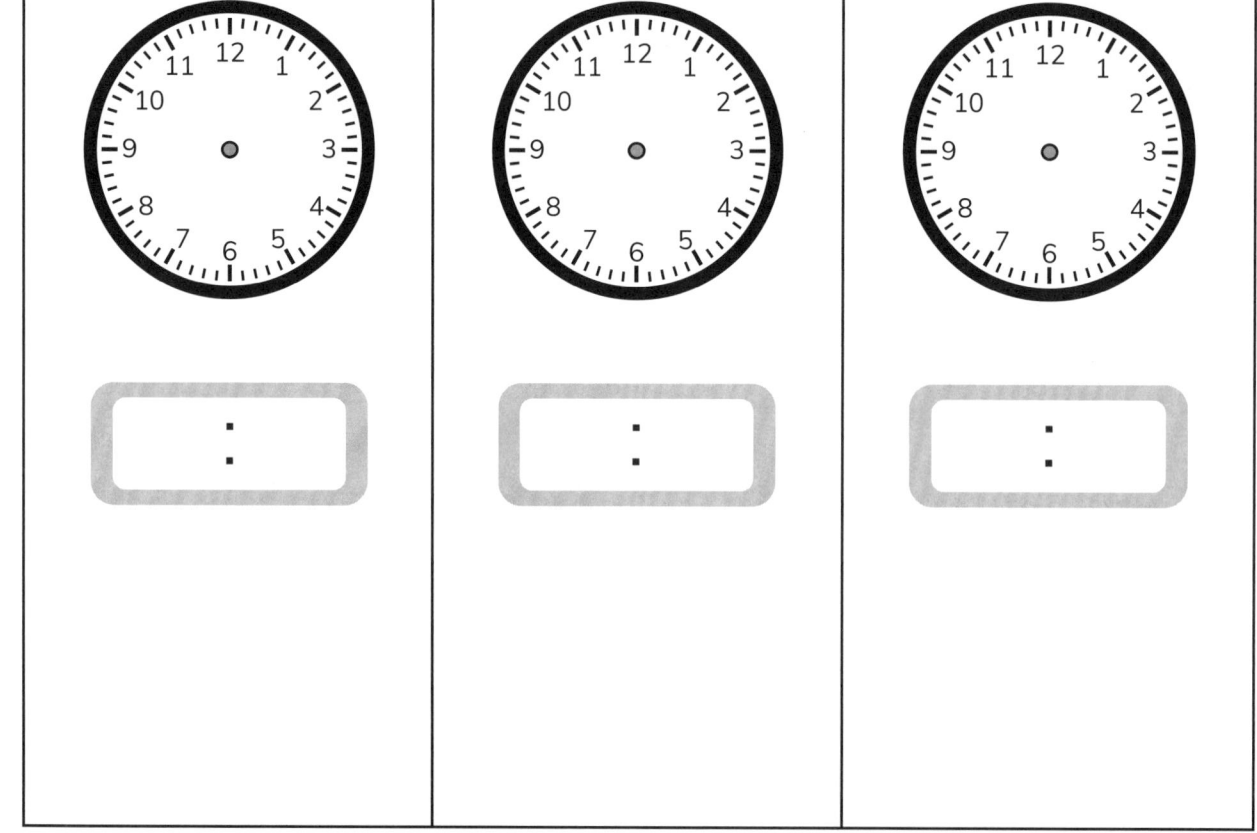

25 to 4

12.1 Telling the time

8  Draw a ring around the odd one out in each row.

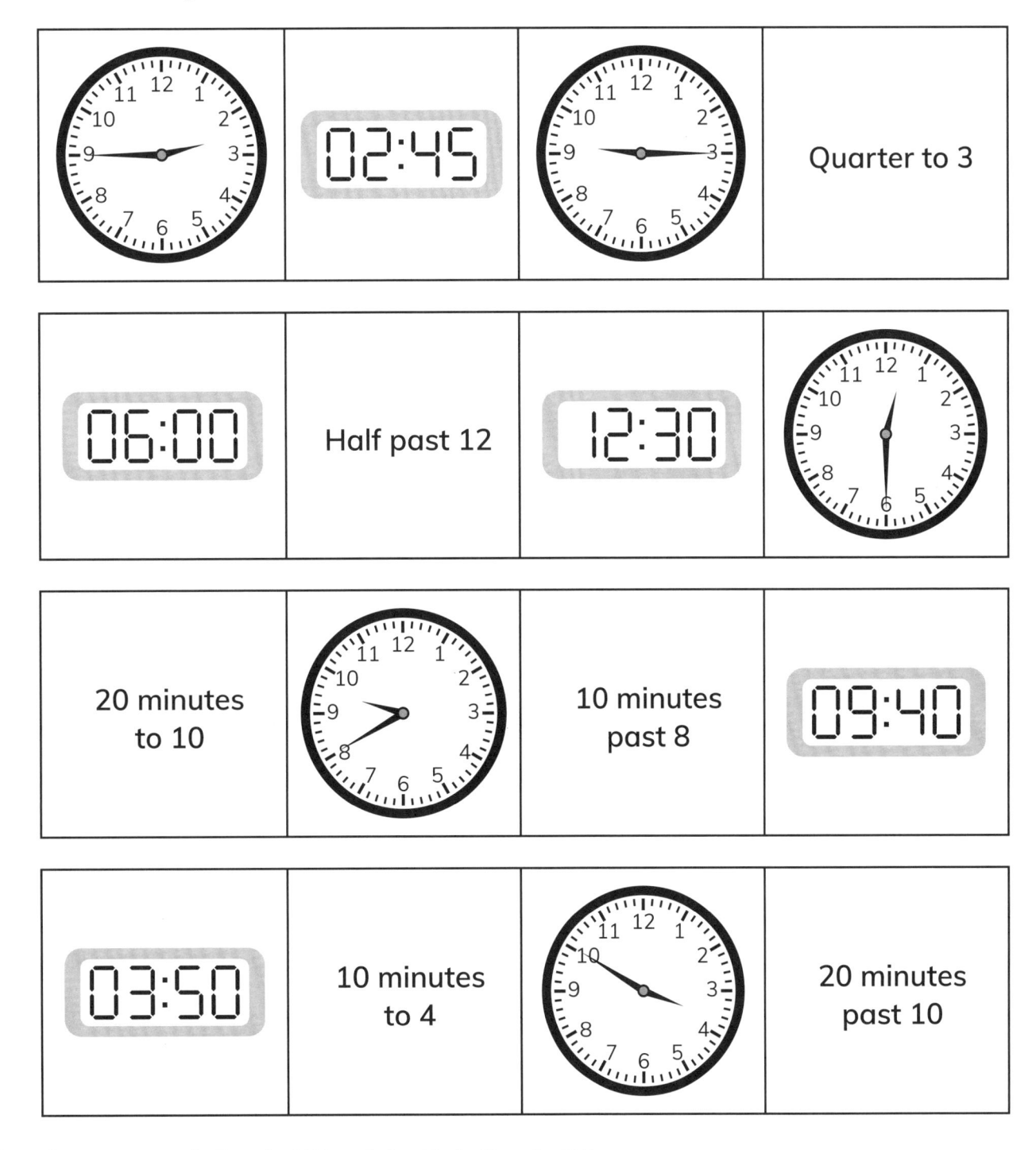

| Clock showing 2:45 | 02:45 | Clock showing 2:45 | Quarter to 3 |

| 06:00 | Half past 12 | 12:30 | Clock showing 12:00 |

| 20 minutes to 10 | Clock showing 8:40 | 10 minutes past 8 | 09:40 |

| 03:50 | 10 minutes to 4 | Clock showing 10:20 | 20 minutes past 10 |

9  A quarter dollar is 25c. A half dollar is 50c.

How could this confuse people when reading the time?

_____

193

# 13 Measures (2)

## > 13.1 Mass and temperature

> gram   kilogram   mass

**Worked example 1**

Arun is making 10 small cakes for his friends.

He needs:

> 8 cups of flour
> 4 cups of sugar
> 2 cups of butter
> 2 eggs

How much of each ingredient does Arun need if he makes 5 small cakes?

Answer:

Arun will need:

   4 cups of flour
   2 cups of sugar
   1 cup of butter
   1 egg

*I will need to halve the amount of ingredients.*

194

13.1 Mass and temperature

## Exercise 13.1

**Focus**

1. Look at the pointer on the scales and answer the questions.

   a  The apple has a mass of 40 grams.

   What is the mass of the pear? _____

   b  The grapes have a mass of 70 grams.
   Draw an arrow to show 70 grams.

   c  One bag of crisps has a mass of 25 grams.
   Draw an arrow to show the mass of 2 bags of crisps.

2. Write the cookie recipe for 2 people if the recipe for 4 people uses:

   100 grams flour

   2 eggs

   50 grams sugar

   _____

   _____

   _____

195

## 13 Measures (2)

3   Estimate and draw a ring around the mass of these objects:

A caterpillar          3 grams          30 grams

A bug                  1 gram           100 grams

3 pencils              15 grams         50 grams

4   Draw arrows on the scales to show the answers.

3 kilograms + 2 kilograms        6 kilograms + 2 kilograms

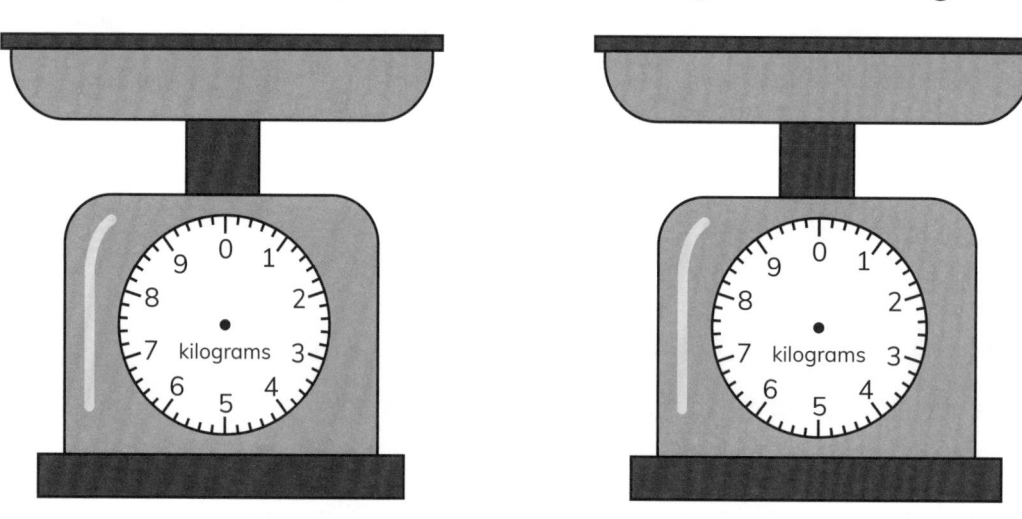

3 kilograms + 3 kilograms + 1 kilograms

13.1 Mass and temperature

5 Find the mass of each animal.

a

2 frogs = _____    1 frog = _____

Draw the scales if you take 1 frog away.

Ring the correct answer:

1 frog is **heavier** than 6 blocks.    1 frog is **lighter** than 6 blocks.

## 13 Measures (2)

b

2 frogs = _____   1 frog = _____

Draw the scales if you take 3 sweets away.

Ring the correct answer:

2 frogs are **heavier** than 5 sweets.    2 frogs are **lighter** than 5 sweets.

13.1 Mass and temperature

c

Draw the scales if another pebble is put in.

Ring the correct answer:

2 pebbles are **heavier** than 1 bird.    2 pebbles are **lighter** than 1 bird.

199

## 13 Measures (2)

6   Zara measures the temperature at 10 o'clock in the morning and again at 3 o'clock in the afternoon. There is a difference of 9 degrees Celsius.

What could the temperatures be?

Write possible answers in the table. The first answer has been completed for you.

| Temperature at 10 o'clock in the morning | Temperature at 3 o'clock in the afternoon |
|---|---|
| 17 | 26 |
|  |  |
|  |  |
|  |  |

## Practice

7   Put these masses in order starting with the lightest.

| 32 grams | 9 grams | 26 grams | 82 grams | 54 grams | 100 grams |

_____  _____  _____  _____  _____  _____

8  Estimate the mass of these objects.
   Draw a ring around the best estimate.

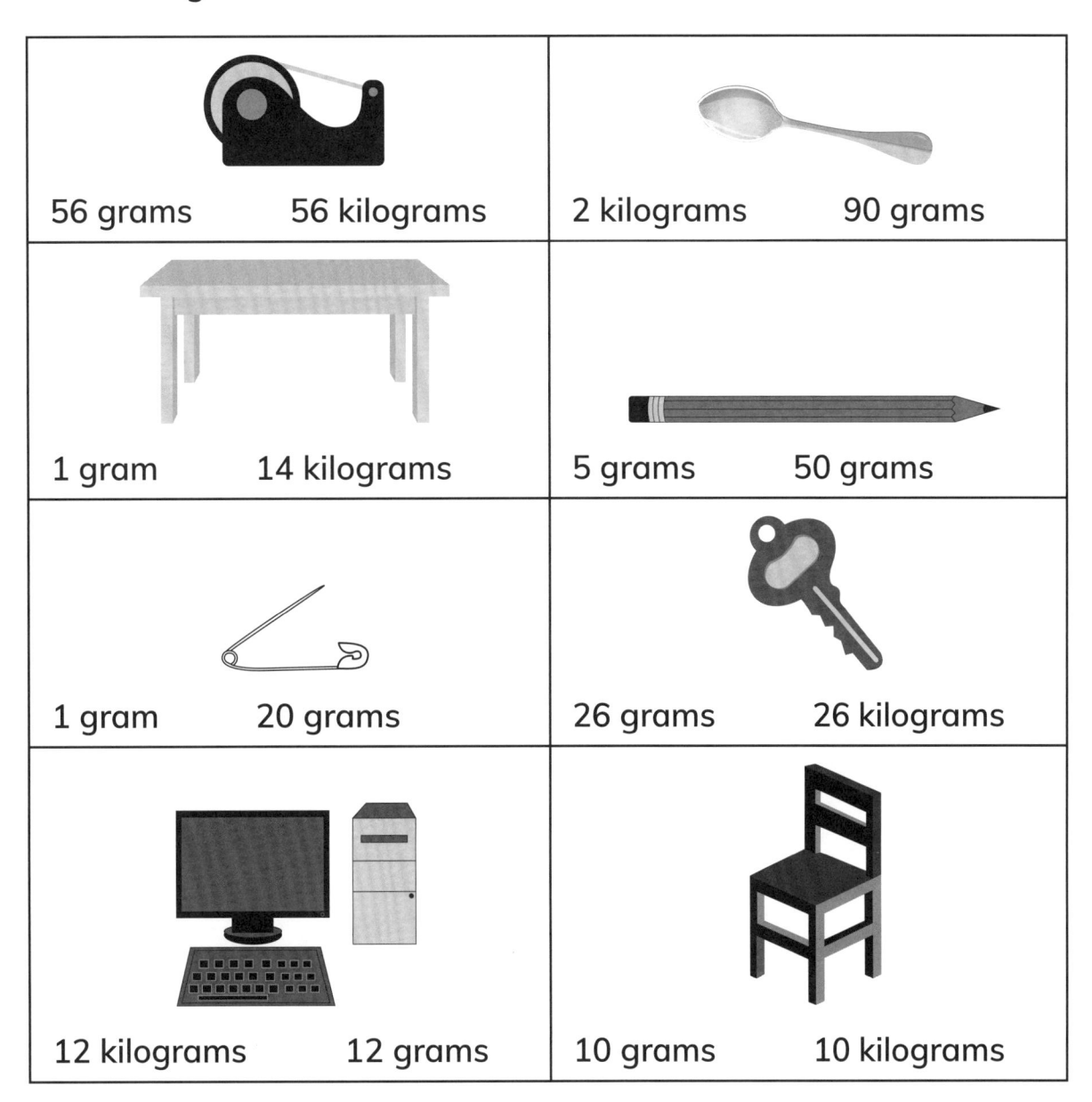

| | |
|---|---|
| 56 grams    56 kilograms | 2 kilograms    90 grams |
| 1 gram    14 kilograms | 5 grams    50 grams |
| 1 gram    20 grams | 26 grams    26 kilograms |
| 12 kilograms    12 grams | 10 grams    10 kilograms |

## 13 Measures (2)

9  Estimate whether these will be more than, less than or about the same as a kilogram.

Put a tick to show your estimate.

Add 2 ideas of your own.

| Object | Less than 1 kilogram | About 1 kilogram | More than 1 kilogram |
|---|---|---|---|
| Brick | | | |
| Baby | | | |
| Cat | | | |
| Mouse | | | |
| Fly | | | |
| | | | |
| | | | |

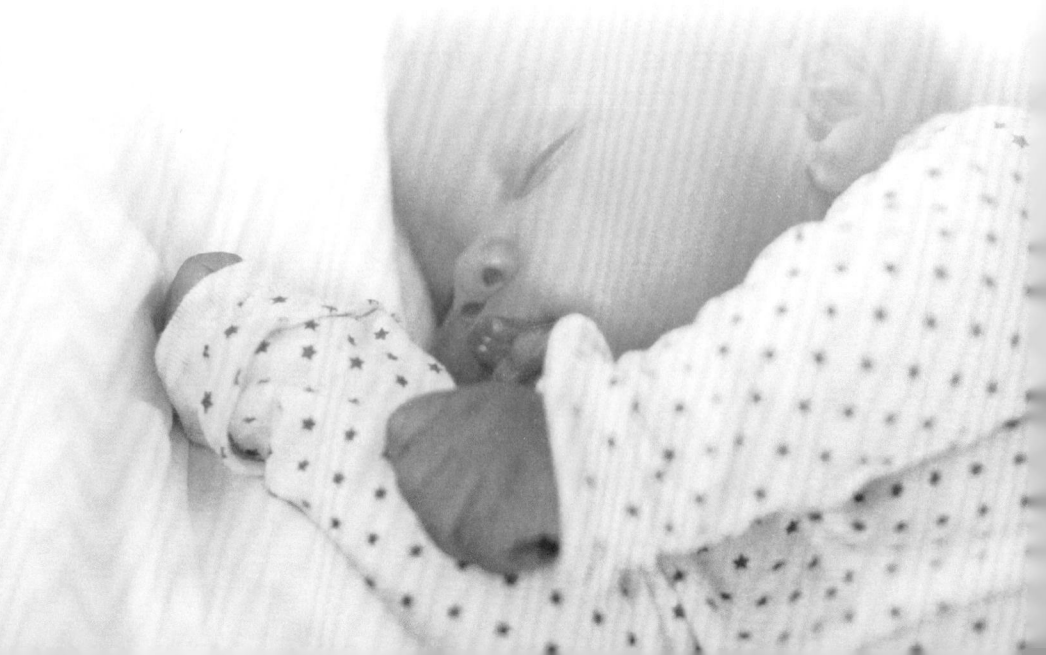

13.1 Mass and temperature

10  Hold 2 objects. Which is heavier? How do you know?

Draw and write what you chose and what you found out.

Are larger objects always heavier than smaller objects?

Draw and write what you have found out.

I am thinking of an object that is heavier than a spoon but lighter than a plate. What could it be?

Draw and write 5 things that it could be.

## 13 Measures (2)

11  If the temperature increases, what happens to the number on the thermometer?

_____

If the temperature decreases, what happens to the number on the thermometer?

_____

Write the temperature shown on each thermometer.

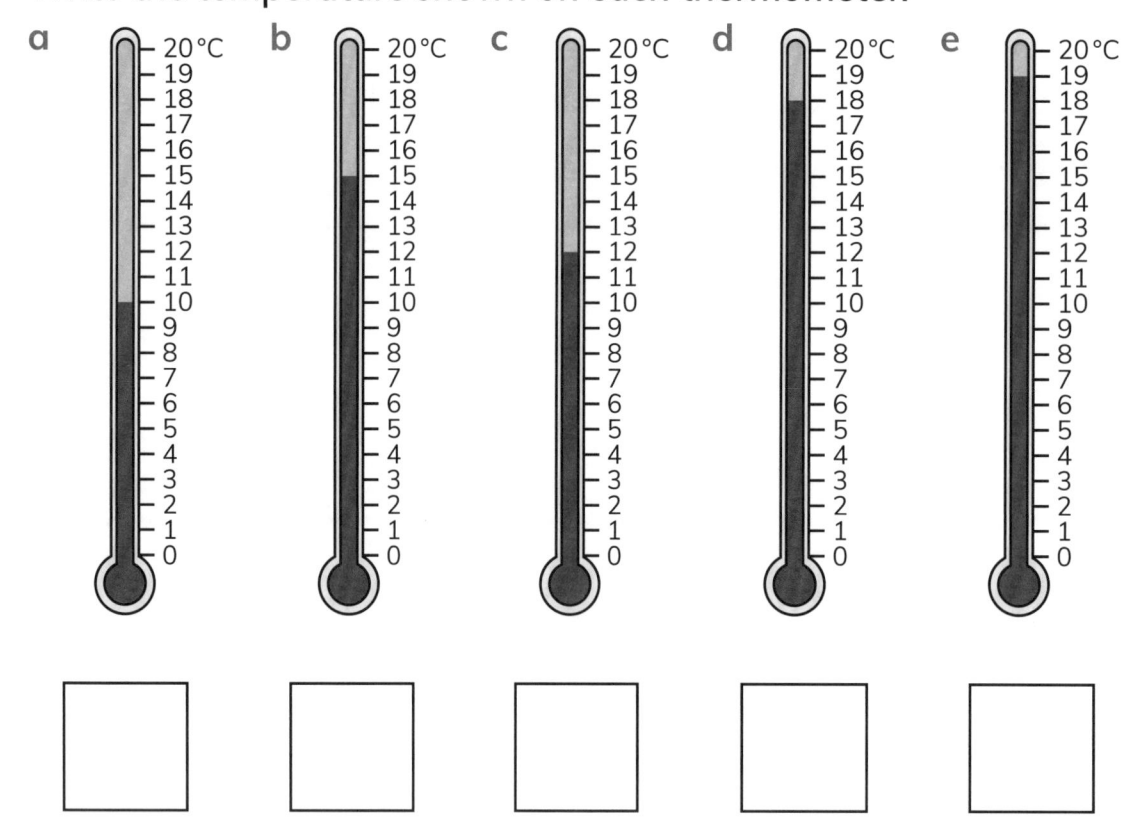

a  b  c  d  e

13.1 Mass and temperature

## Challenge

12 Experiment with some scales and find 2 objects that have about the same mass.

Do this 3 times using different objects.

Record what you have found out.

_____

_____

_____

13 What is the mass of each box?

Write your answer using kilograms.

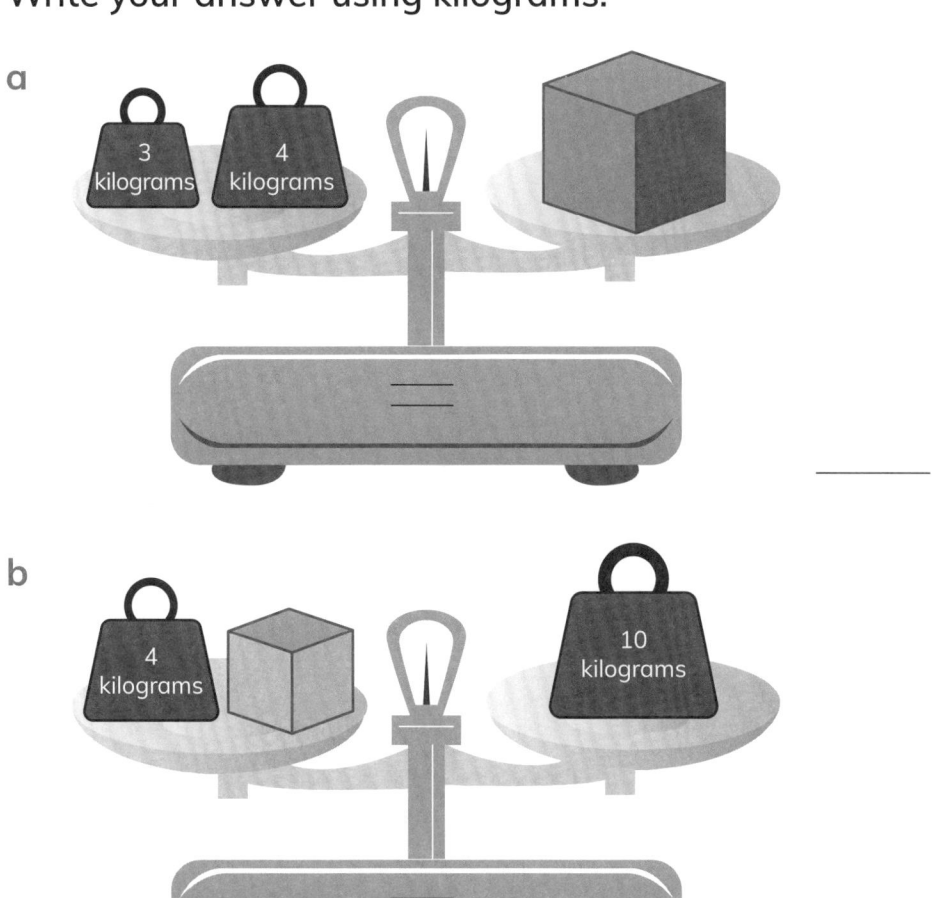

a

_____

b

_____

**13** Measures (2)

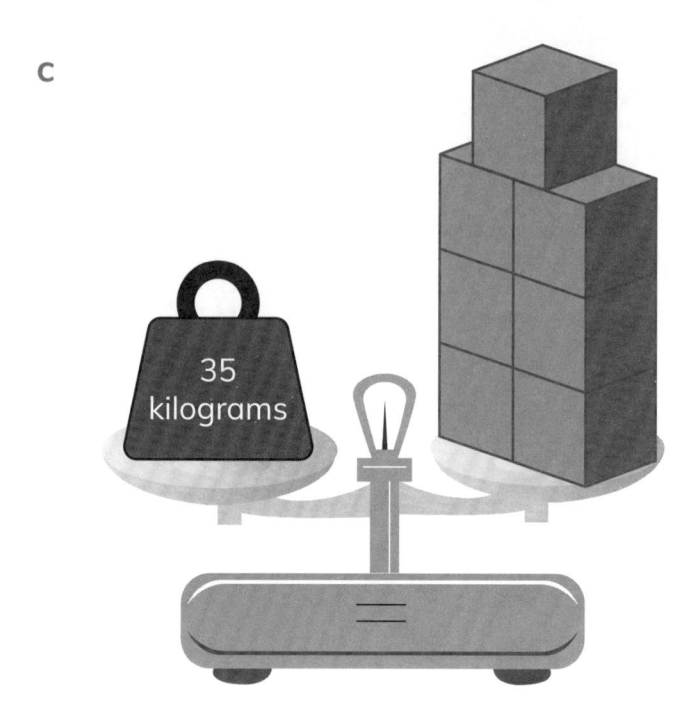

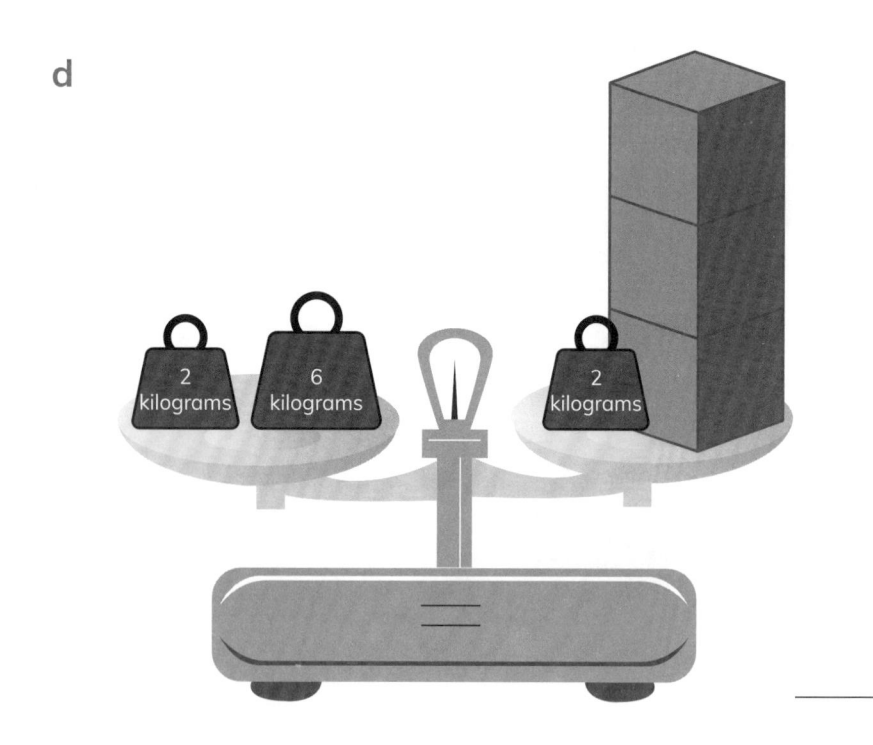

c

d

13.1 Mass and temperature

14  You have these weights.

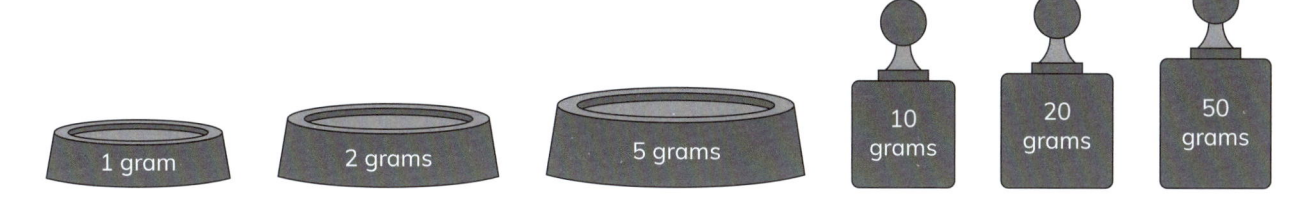

1 gram   2 grams   5 grams   10 grams   20 grams   50 grams

You have these fruits.

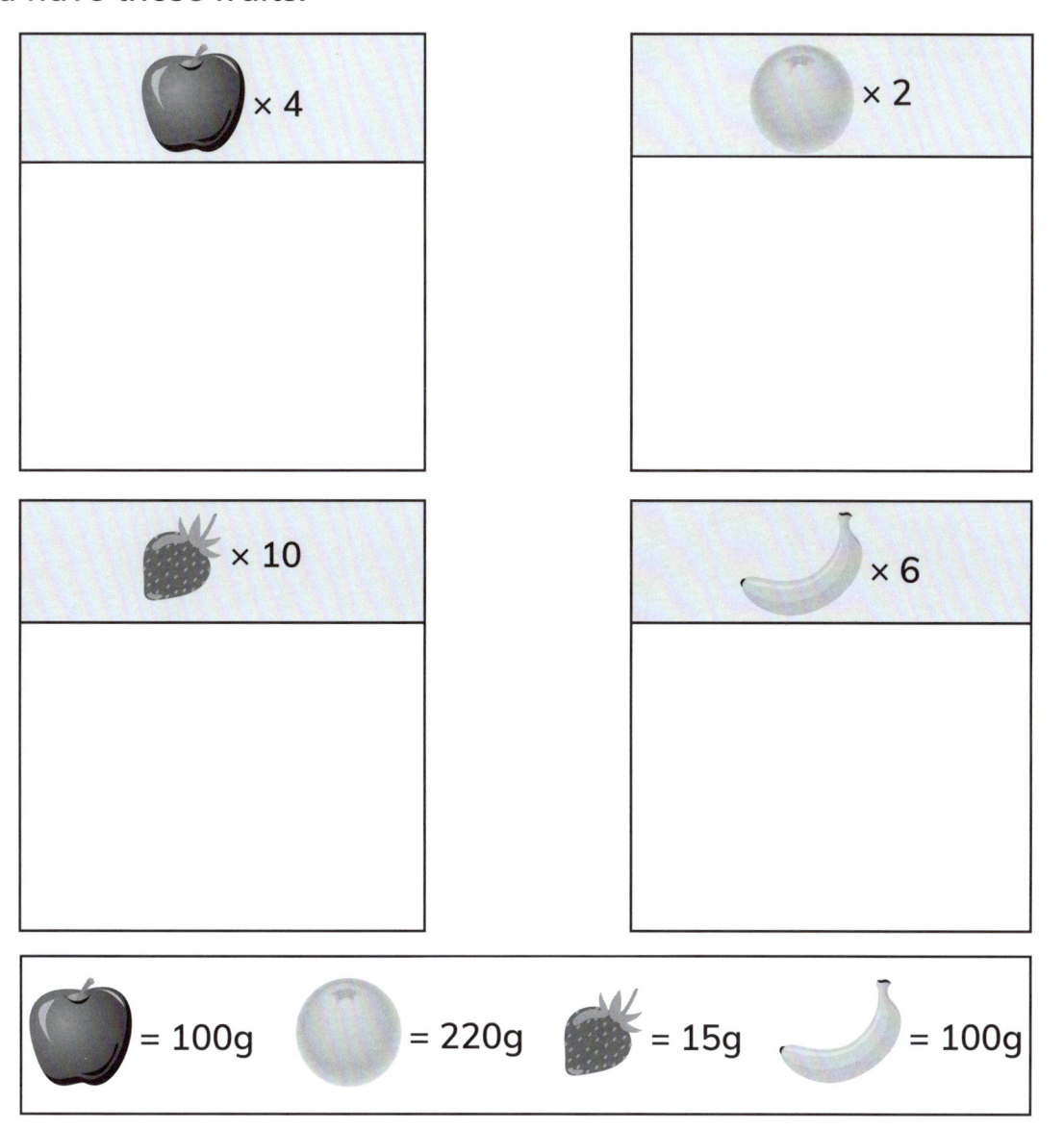

× 4

× 2

× 10

× 6

🍎 = 100g    🍊 = 220g    🍓 = 15g    🍌 = 100g

How many different ways can you make the total mass of the fruit in each box?

Find 2 ways for each fruit. Draw or write your answers in each box.

You can use the weights more than once.

207

## 13 Measures (2)

15  a  One apple weighs 10 cubes.

How many cubes will balance 1 pineapple? ☐

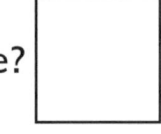

Explain how you know.

_____

_____

b  2 bananas weigh 12 cubes.

How many cubes will balance 1 pear? ☐

Explain how you know.

_____

_____

Write your own mass problem and the answer.

_____

_____

_____

13.1 Mass and temperature

16  What is the same and what is different about these thermometers?

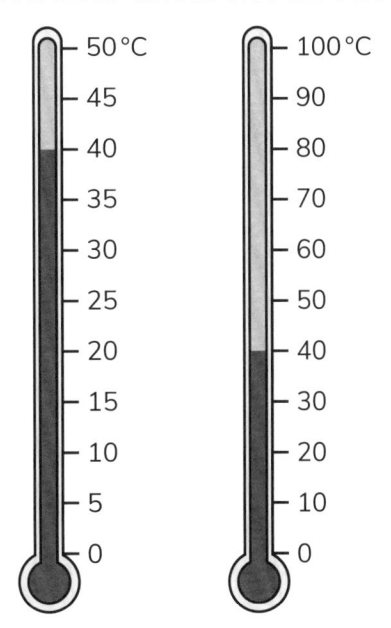

___

Show the temperature on each thermometer.

a) 5 degrees Celsius

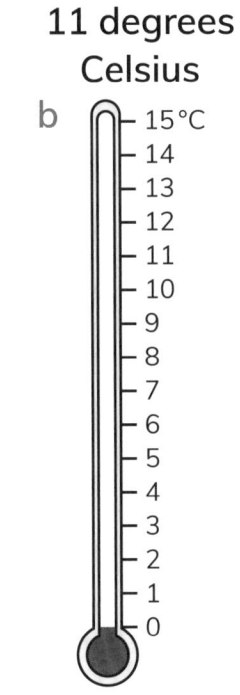

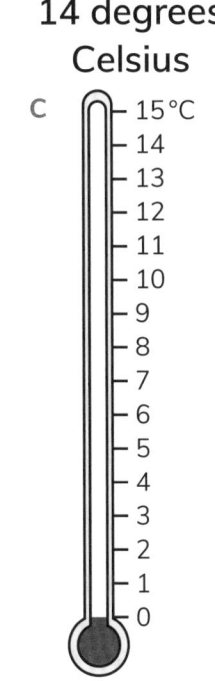

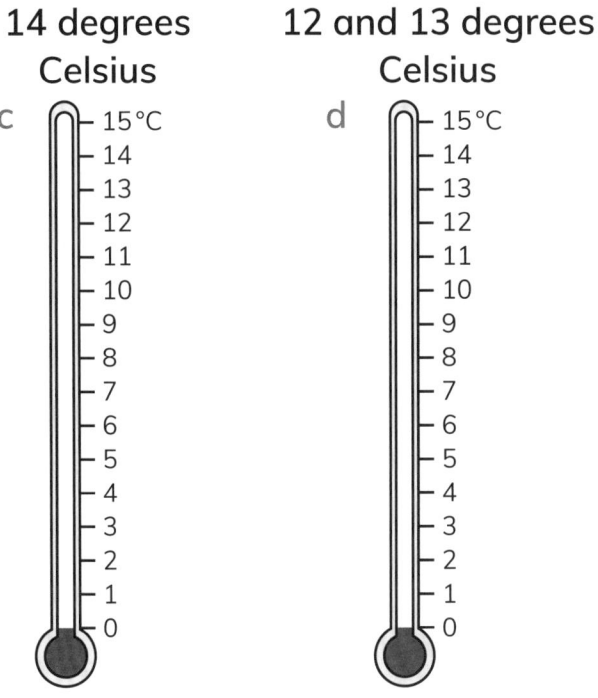

b) 11 degrees Celsius

c) 14 degrees Celsius

d) half way between 12 and 13 degrees Celsius

# 13 Measures (2)

## > 13.2 Capacity

### Exercise 13.2

**Focus**

capacity   litre   millilitre

**Worked example 2**

Compare the amounts of water.

Use the words in the boxes to label the bottles.

| Empty | Half full | Full | Almost full | Almost empty |

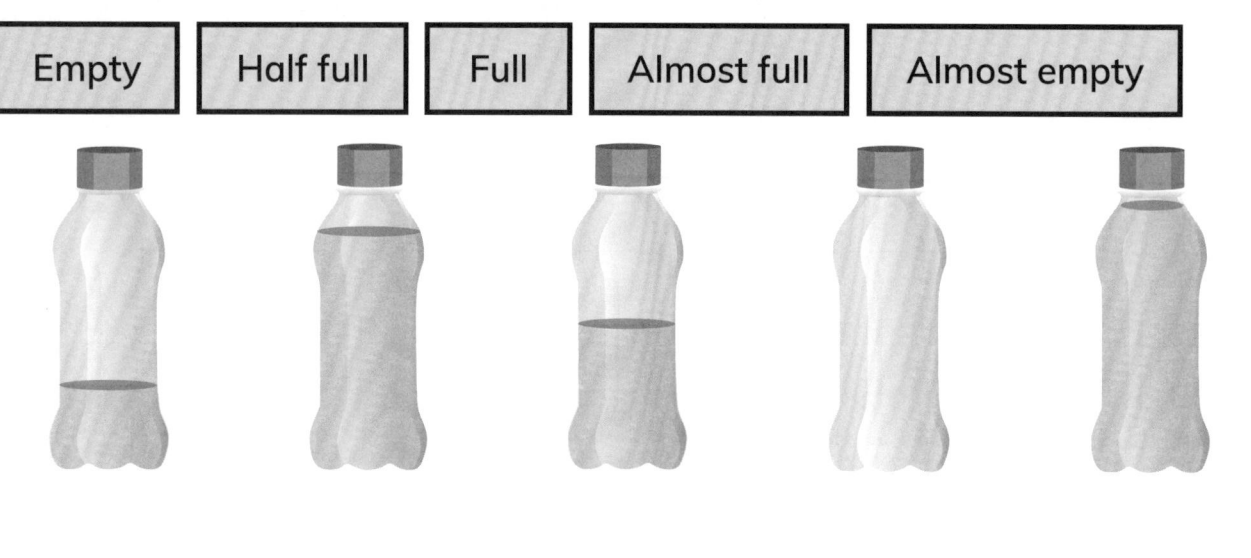

*Look at the amount of water in each bottle. Which one shall we start with?*

*I think it is a good idea to start with the full and empty bottles.*

13.2 Capacity

**Continued**

Full   Empty   Half full                     Almost full   Almost empty

"The one that is half full is easy."

"That just leaves the last two, almost full and almost empty."

1   Compare the amounts of water.

   Write 'more' or 'less' in the boxes.

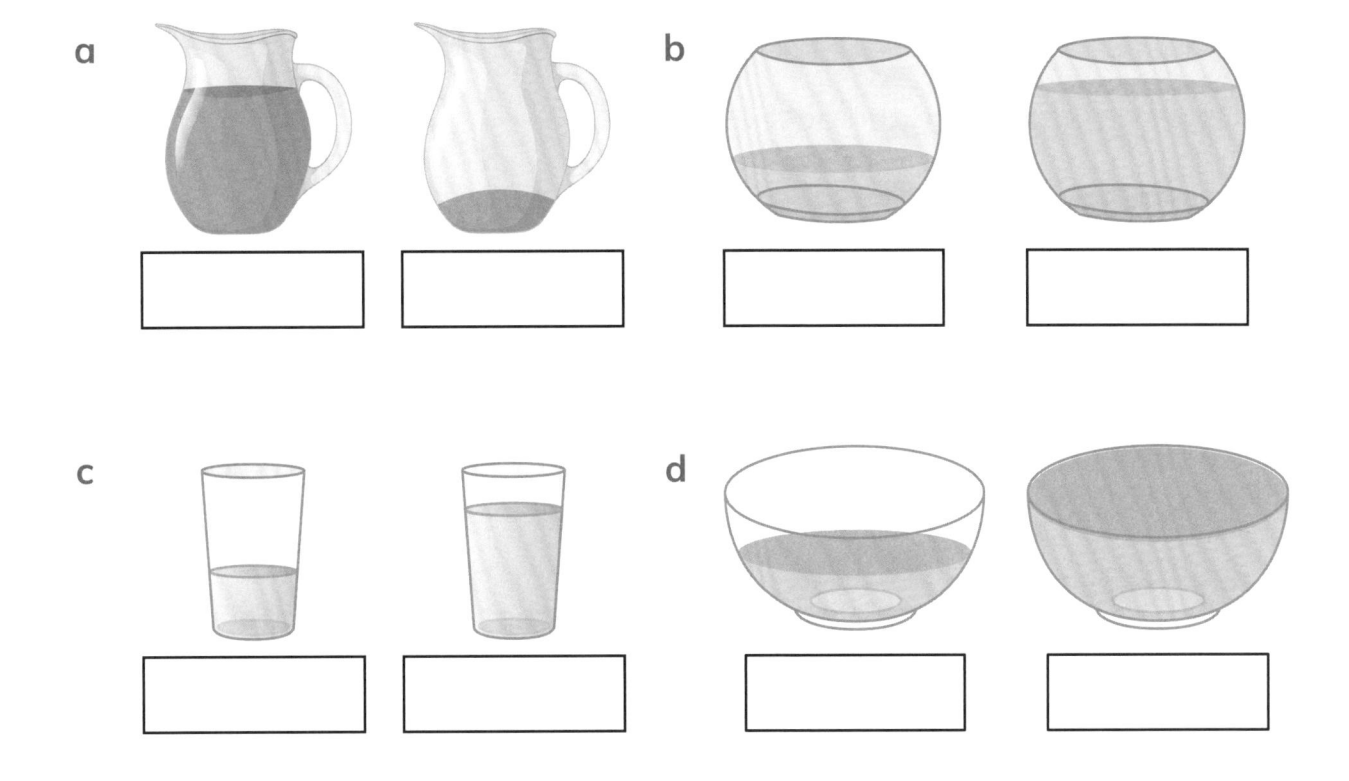

   a

   b

   c

   d

211

## 13 Measures (2)

2  When these containers are full, do they hold more or less than 1 litre? Draw a ring around the answer.

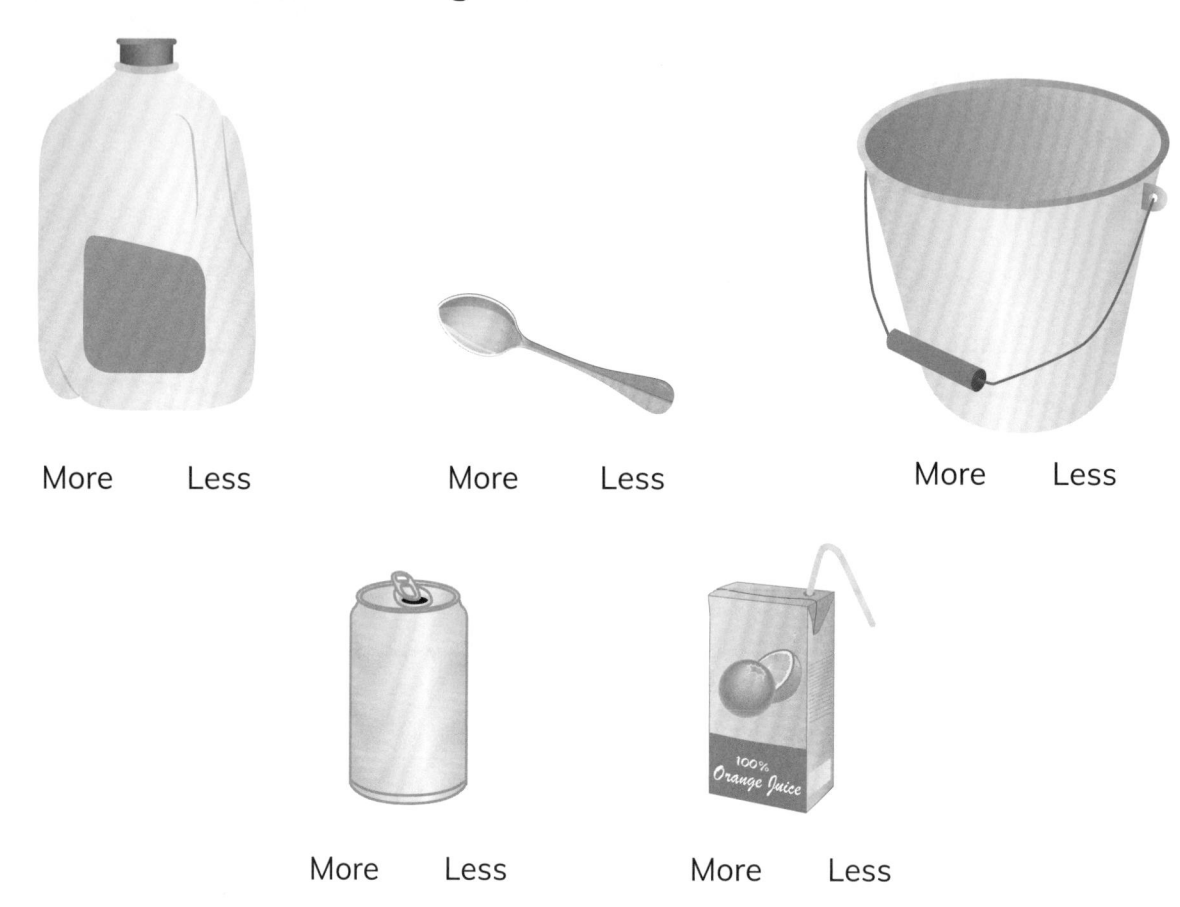

More    Less           More    Less           More    Less

More    Less           More    Less

3  Draw a ring around the best estimate.

2 litres        1 litre         $\frac{1}{2}$ litre

2 litres        1 litre         $\frac{1}{2}$ litre

2 litres        5 litres        10 litres

4  This bottle holds 1 litre of water.

A millilitre is about 20 drops of water.

Draw a ring around the correct answer.

|  | Litres | Millilitres |
|---|---|---|
| (bucket) | 9 litres | 9 millilitres |
| (orange juice bottle) | 1 litre | 1 millilitre |
| (fish tank) | 50 litres | 50 millilitres |

## 13 Measures (2)

## Practice

5. Sofia's jar is wide and holds 5 litres. Sofia fills her jar with water so that it is full.

   Sofia pours the water from her wide jar into a tall jar. The tall jar only holds 3 litres.

   How much water is left over?

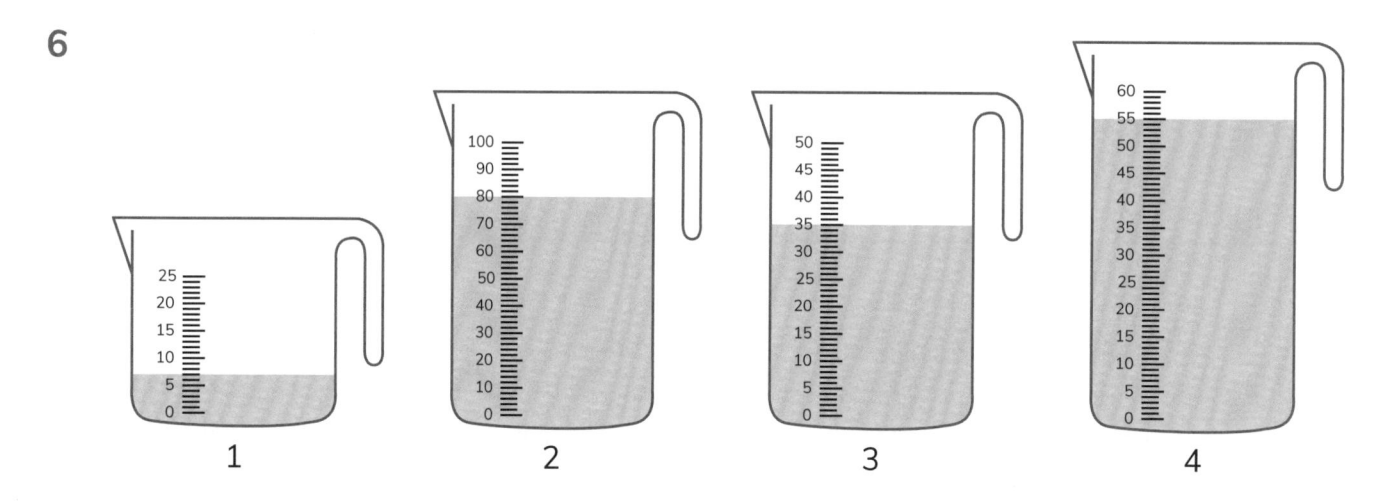

6. 

   How many millilitres in each jug?

## Challenge

7. Three learners need their water bottles filled. Each bottle holds half of a litre. The teacher has a full 2 and a half litre bottle.

   Does she have enough water?

   Is there any left?

   How much?

13.2 Capacity

8  Marcus collects some rain water in a bucket that holds 6 and a half litres. The bucket is full.

He uses 3 and a half litres to water some plants. How much is left?

Yesterday he used a 7 litre bucket to collect the same amount of rain water.

How much more rain is needed to fill this bucket?

9  For each bottle, find out how many times it takes to fill each of the bigger bottles.

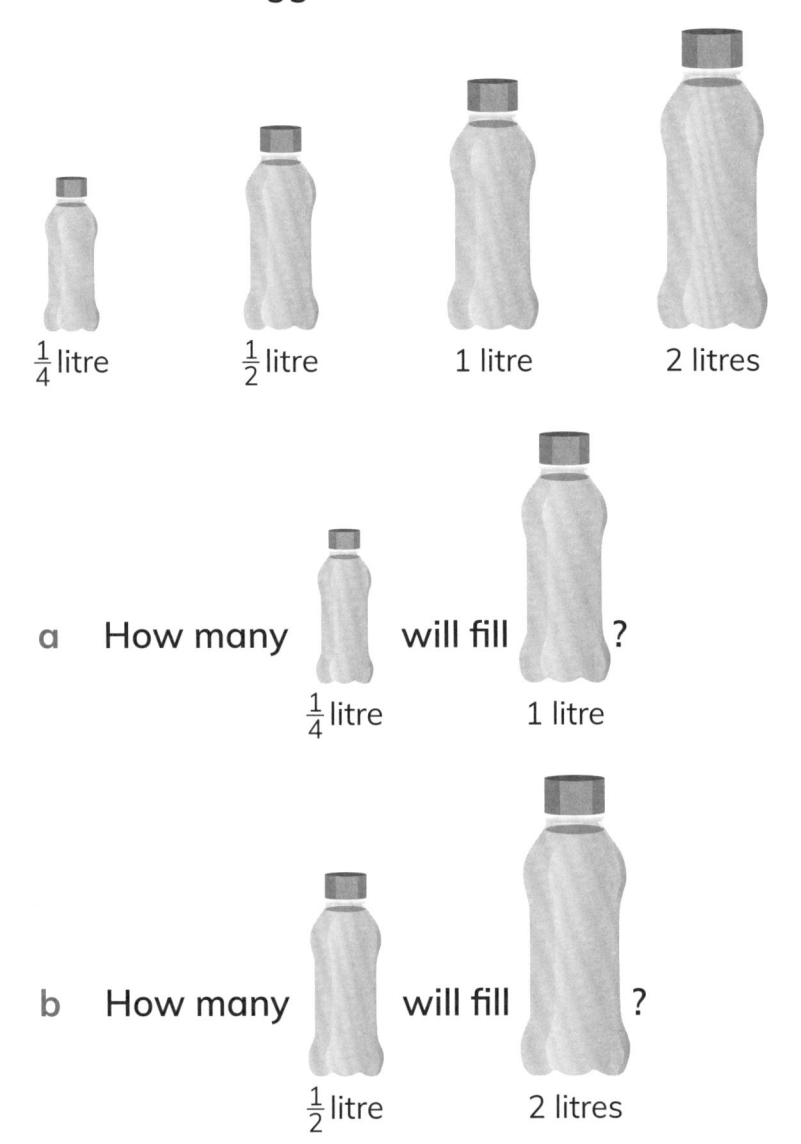

$\frac{1}{4}$ litre     $\frac{1}{2}$ litre     1 litre     2 litres

**Tip**

You do not need to use water. Look at the capacity.

a  How many $\frac{1}{4}$ litre will fill 1 litre ?

b  How many $\frac{1}{2}$ litre will fill 2 litres ?

## 13 Measures (2)

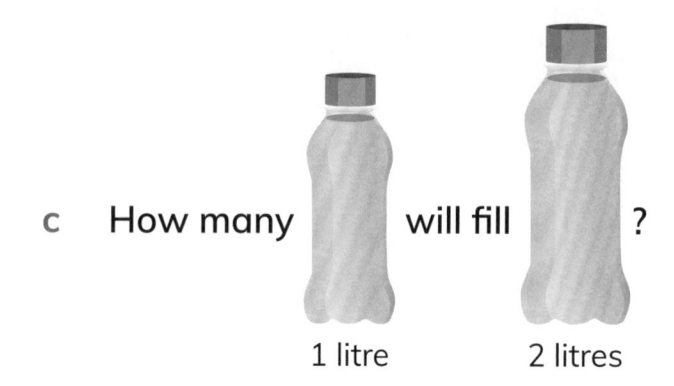

c How many ![1 litre bottle] will fill ![2 litres bottle] ?

                      1 litre        2 litres

10 Show these amounts on the measuring cylinders.

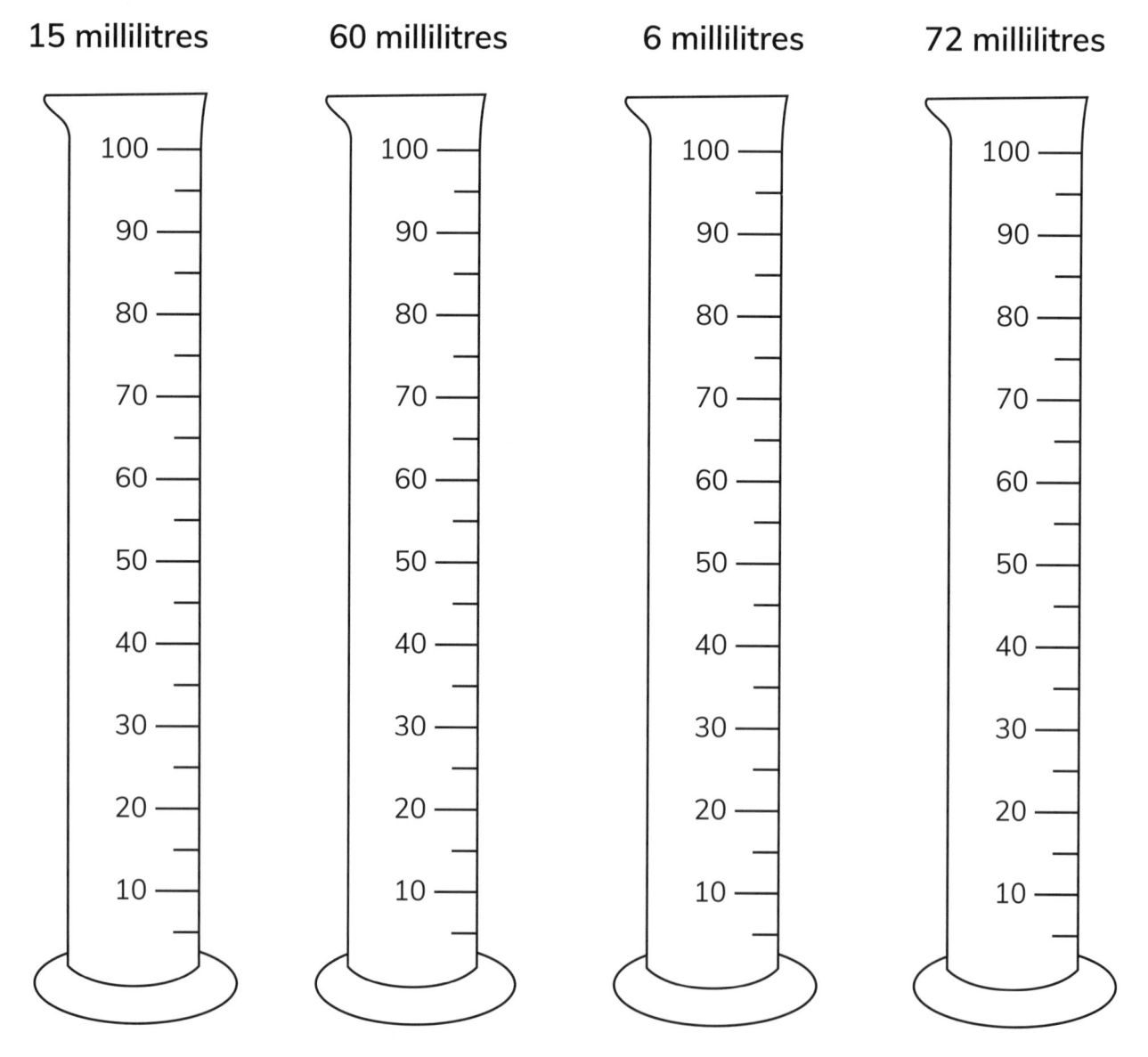

15 millilitres      60 millilitres      6 millilitres      72 millilitres

# 14 Pattern and probability

## > 14.1 Pattern and probability

**Exercise 14.1**

**Focus**

> chance    experiment    outcome
> probability    random    regular pattern

**Worked example 1**

What is the difference between a regular pattern and a random sequence?

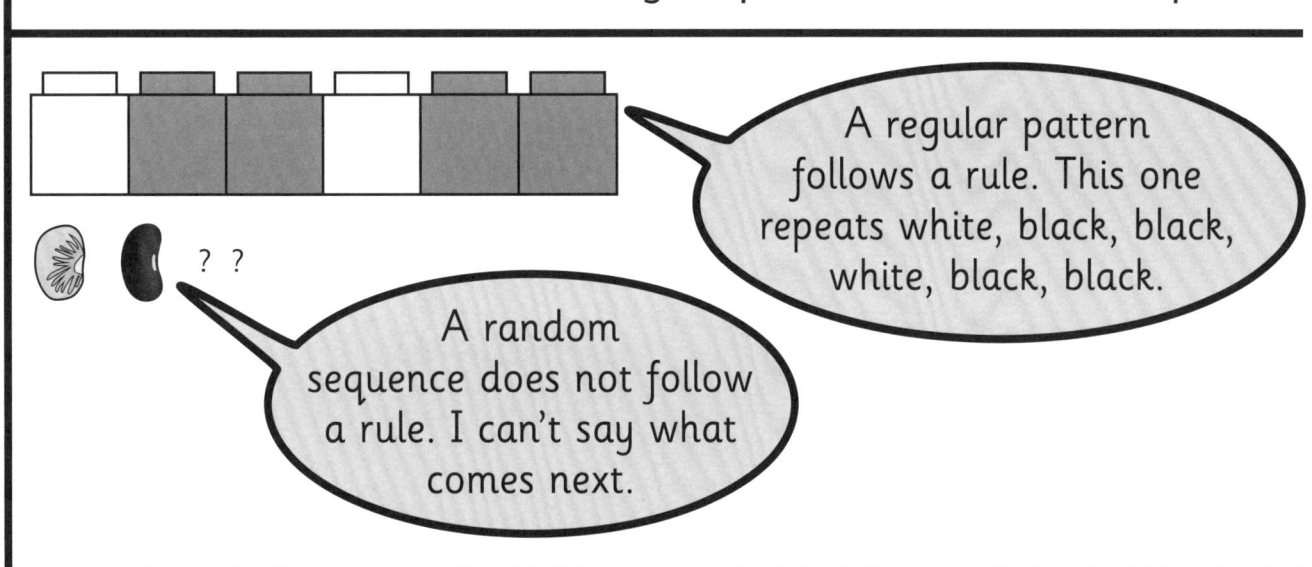

> A regular pattern follows a rule. This one repeats white, black, black, white, black, black.

> A random sequence does not follow a rule. I can't say what comes next.

1  Complete these regular patterns.

## 14 Pattern and probability

**2** Make 2 different random sequences using 2 different colours.

| | | | | | | | | | |
|---|---|---|---|---|---|---|---|---|---|

| | | | | | | | | | |
|---|---|---|---|---|---|---|---|---|---|

Make a regular pattern using 2 different colours.

| | | | | | | | | | |
|---|---|---|---|---|---|---|---|---|---|

**3** Without looking, Yusuf picks an object from the jar.
What could he have picked? Ring all answers.

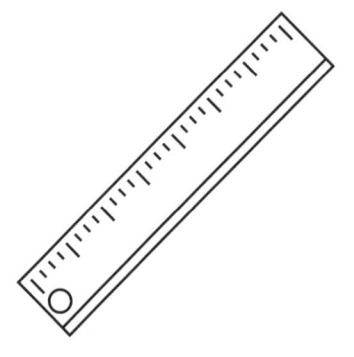

14.1 Pattern and probability

## Practice

4   You need 10 objects, 5 of one colour and 5 of another.

You could use counters, marbles or other small items.

Put them all in a container.

Without looking, take an object out of the container.

Take a second object.

What did you get?

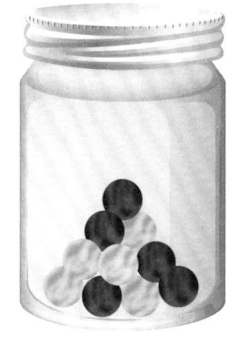

_____

Take two more objects. Do you always get the same colour?

_____

Write or draw what you did and what you found out.

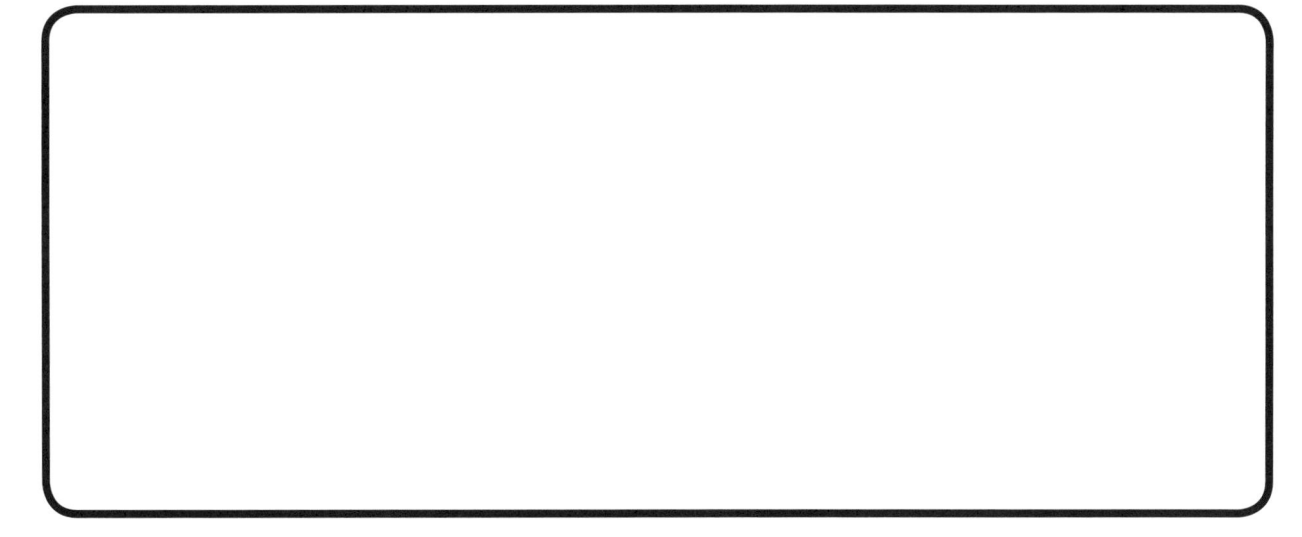

Predict and describe the results if the experiment was repeated.
Would they be the same or different? Give your reasons.

_____

_____

## 14 Pattern and probability

5. Using a pencil, hold a paper clip at the centre of the spinner.

   Spin the paper clip. What number does it land on?
   Is the number odd or even? Spin the paper clip 10 times.

   Colour the chart to show your results.

   Which did you land on the most, odd or even numbers?

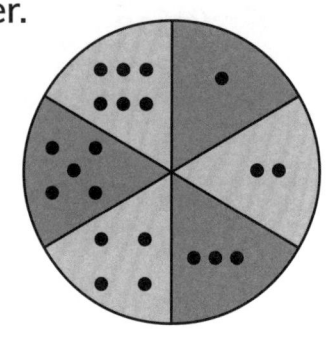

   |     |      |
   | --- | ---- |
   |     |      |
   |     |      |
   |     |      |
   |     |      |
   |     |      |
   |     |      |
   |     |      |
   |     |      |
   |     |      |
   |     |      |
   | **Odd** | **Even** |

   What did you notice?

   _____

   You could do this again and see if your results are the same.

6  A repeating pattern uses black, white and grey objects.

   Draw two possible patterns.

   ![blank box]

## Challenge

7  Make 2 different regular patterns using 3 different colours.

   | | | | | | | | | | |
   |---|---|---|---|---|---|---|---|---|---|
   | | | | | | | | | | |

   | | | | | | | | | | |
   |---|---|---|---|---|---|---|---|---|---|
   | | | | | | | | | | |

   Draw a random sequence using the same colours as before.

   | | | | | | | | | | |
   |---|---|---|---|---|---|---|---|---|---|
   | | | | | | | | | | |

   Where would you see a regular pattern?

   _____

   Where would you see a random sequence?

   _____

## 14 Pattern and probability

8  You will need a small square of paper or card.

Draw a cross on one side and leave the other side blank.

Hold the paper at arms length and let it drop to the ground.

Which side is showing?

_____

Do this 10 times.

Record the results in the table using tally marks.

| Cross | |
|---|---|
| No cross | |

Do it 10 times again. Do you get the same results? Why?

_____

_____

9  Describe the sequence.

☐ △ ⬠ ☐ ▭ ⬠ ☐ ◯ ⬠

_____

_____

# 15 Symmetry, position and movement

> 15.1 Symmetry, position and movement

Exercise 15.1

**Focus**

> anticlockwise   clockwise
> equivalent   mirror line
> reflection   reverse

**Worked example 1**

Use the mirror line to make a symmetrical picture.

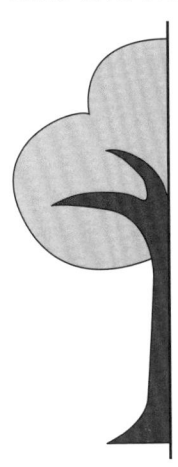

223

## 15 Symmetry, position and movement

**Continued**

How do you know it's symmetrical?

I draw some of the shape. Then I use a mirror to check that it is symmetrical.

1. Use the mirror line to make a symmetrical picture.

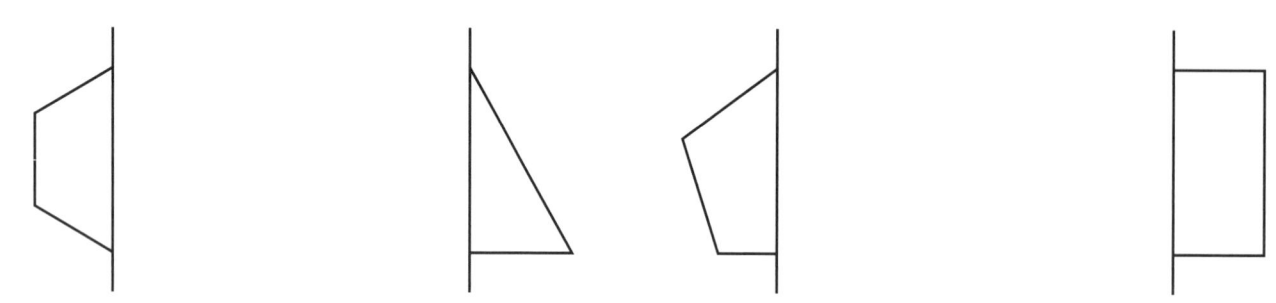

15.1 Symmetry, position and movement

2   Look at each shape.

Tick what it will look like when it has turned clockwise one quarter turn:

a

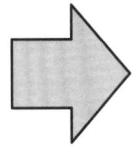

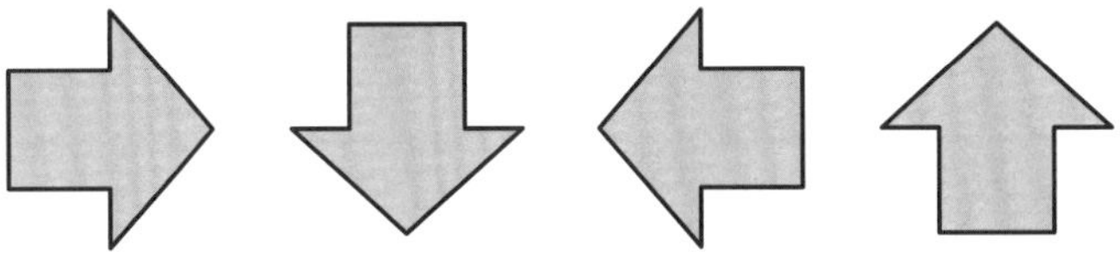

b

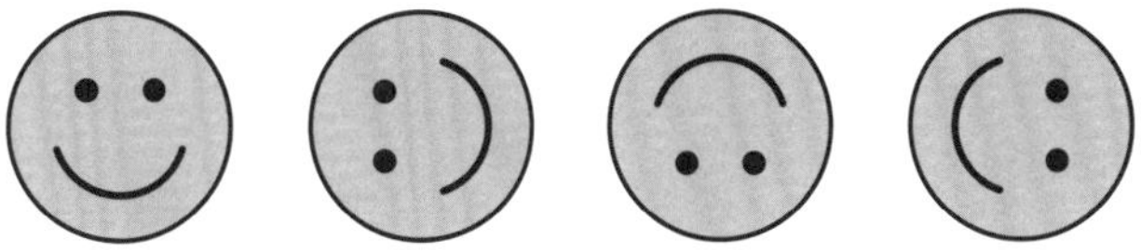

3   The minute hand makes these turns. It starts at 12.

What number does it stop on?

a    Half a turn anticlockwise

b    Half a turn clockwise

c    1 quarter turn clockwise

d    1 quarter turn anticlockwise

## 15 Symmetry, position and movement

**Practice**

4. Draw more than one 4-sided shape that has a vertical line of symmetry.

5. Look at each shape.

    Tick what it will look like when it has turned clockwise one half turn.

    a

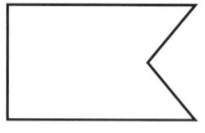

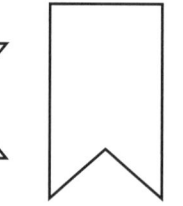

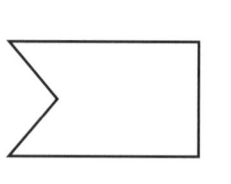

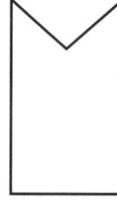

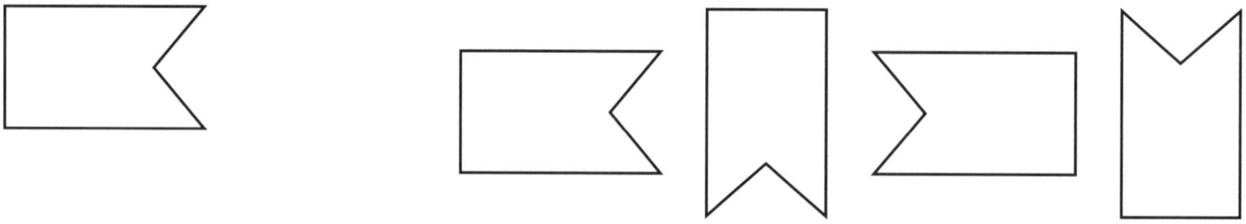

    b

15.1 Symmetry, position and movement

6   The minute hand makes these turns. It starts at 6.
    What number does it stop on? Draw the hand on each clock.
    Colour the matching clocks that show the same number.
    Did they have the same instruction?

A full turn clockwise

Half a turn clockwise

Half a turn anticlockwise

A quarter turn clockwise

A quarter turn anticlockwise

A full turn anticlockwise

15 Symmetry, position and movement

## Challenge

7 Draw a mirror line on these shapes.

Draw 2 pictures of your own and show the mirror lines.

15.1 Symmetry, position and movement

8 Draw what you think these shapes will look like when they have turned.

Anticlockwise a quarter turn

Clockwise a quarter turn

What do you notice?

Clockwise a half turn

Anticlockwise a half turn

What do you notice?

9 Draw each shape after a quarter turn clockwise.

Clockwise a quarter turn

Clockwise a quarter turn

# 15 Symmetry, position and movement

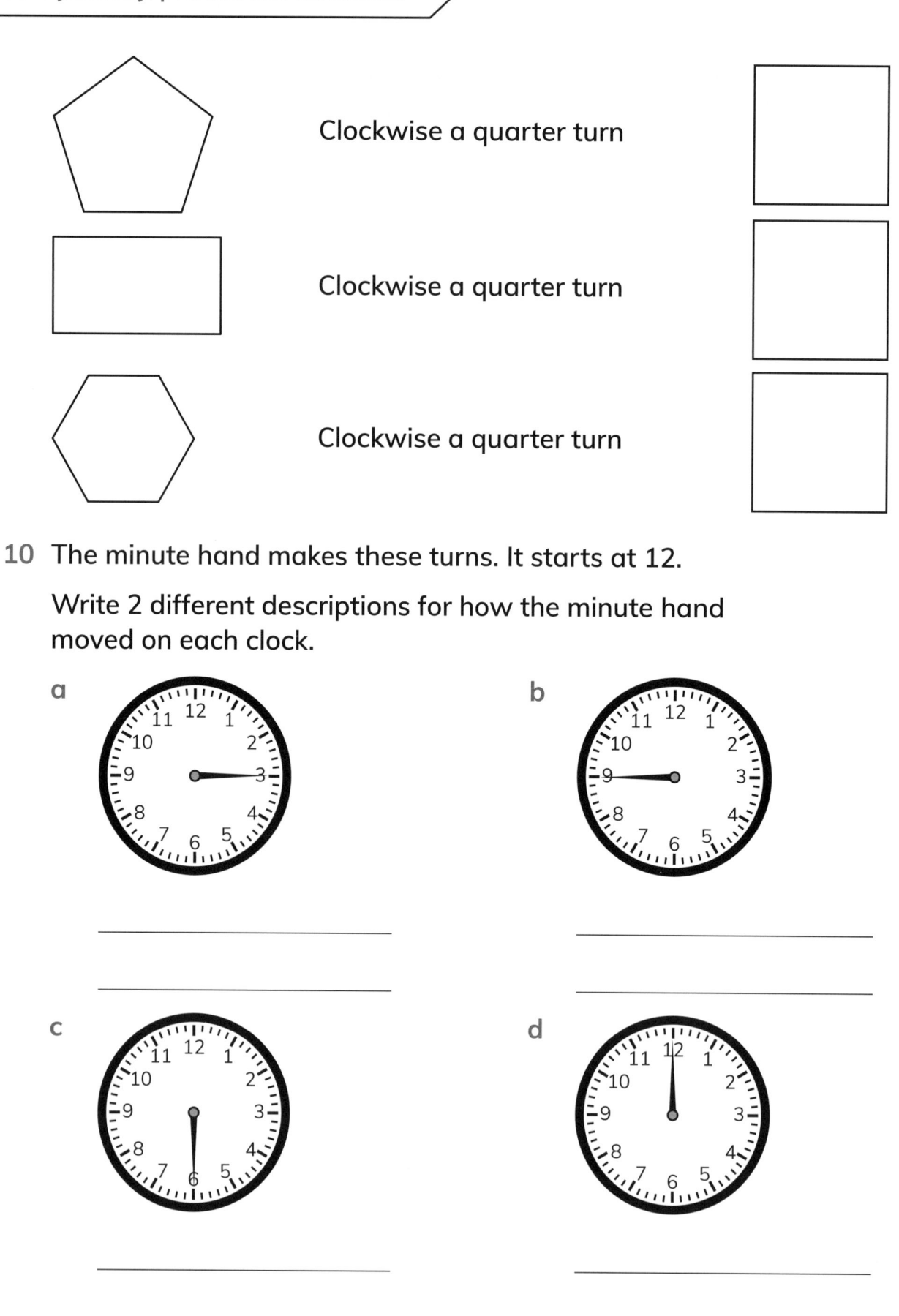

Clockwise a quarter turn

Clockwise a quarter turn

Clockwise a quarter turn

10 The minute hand makes these turns. It starts at 12.

Write 2 different descriptions for how the minute hand moved on each clock.

a

b

c

d

# Acknowledgements

It takes an extraordinary number of people to put together a new series of resources and their comments, support and encouragement have been really important to us. We would like to thank the following people: Philip Rees and Veronica Wastell for the support they have given the authors; Lynne McClure for her feedback and comments on early sections of the manuscript; Thomas Carter, Caroline Walton, Laura Collins, Charlotte Griggs, Gabby Martin, Elizabeth Scurfield, Berenice Howard-Smith, Jo Burling, Zohir Naciri, Emma McCrea and Eddie Rippeth as part of the team at Cambridge preparing the resources. We would also like to particularly thank all of the anonymous reviewers for their time and comments on the manuscript and as part of the endorsement process.

*The authors and publishers acknowledge the following sources of copyright material and are grateful for the permissions granted. While every effort has been made, it has not always been possible to identify the sources of all the material used, or to trace all copyright holders. If any omissions are brought to our notice, we will be happy to include the appropriate acknowledgements on reprinting.*

*Thanks to the following for permission to reproduce images:*

Cover Photo: Pablo Gallego (Beehive Illustration)

Mohamad Faizal Ramli / EyeEm / Getty Images; samxmeg / Getty Images; jyu-akc / Getty Images; busypix / Getty Images; Photodisc / Getty Images; Nattawut Lakjit / EyeEm / Getty Images; Image Source / Getty Images; Jesper Klausen / Science Photo Library / Getty Images; artcyclone / Getty Images; Veerapong Boonporn / EyeEm / Getty Images; Jenny Dettrick / Getty Images; By Nada Stankova Photography / Getty Images; MerveKarahan / Getty Images; Aekkarak Thongjiew / EyeEm / Getty Images; Karl Tapales / Getty Images; AJ_Watt / Getty Images; Image Source / Getty Images; Sebastian Condrea / Getty Images; imamember/Getty Images; eustockimages / Getty Images; Richard Drury / Getty Images; Ricardo Liberato / Getty Images; Neha Gupta / Getty Images; Yulia Reznikov / Getty Images; Jenny Dettrick / Getty Images; Dilok Klaisataporn / EyeEm / Getty Images; Gabriel Visintin / EyeEm / Getty Images; Fountain_of_useless_info / Getty Images; Klaus Vartzbed / EyeEm / Getty Images; hdere / Getty Images; mikroman6 / Getty Images; Carmen Martínez Torrón / Getty Images; David Malan / Getty Images